THE MEN WHO MARCHED AWAY

Canada's Infantry in World War I
1914 - 1918

The Vanwell History Project Series

THE MEN WHO MARCHED AWAY

Canada's Infantry in World War I
1914 - 1918

R. James Steel
Project Consultant: Don Revell

Vanwell Publishing Limited
St. Catharines, Ontario

Dedication

To my grandchildren:
Robert James, Callum James, and Jessica Marie.

Canadian Cataloguing in Publication Data

Steel, R. J.
  The men who marched away

(Vanwell history project series)
Includes bibliographical references.
ISBN 0-920277-56-X

1. Canada. 2. Canadian Army – History – World War, 1914 - 1918 – Juvenile literature. 2. World War, 1914 - 1918 – Canada – Juvenile literature. 3. World War, 1914 - 1918 – Campaigns – Western – Juvenile literature. I. Title II. Series.

D547.C2S84 1989   940.4'12'71   C89-094882-8

Copyright 1989 by R. James Steel.© All rights reserved. No part of this publication may be reproduced, stored in a retrieval system, or transmitted in any form without the written permission of the Publisher.

ISN 0-920277-56-X
Maps by Loris Gasparotto
Cover photograph National Archives of Canada
Design Susan Nicholson
Printed and Bound by John Deyell Company

CONTENTS

Chapter One
9
Canada's Call to Arms

Chapter Two
15
Baptism of Fire

Chapter Three
21
Canada Carries On: May - December 1915

Chapter Four
29
Holding the Line

Chapter Five
35
The Battle of the Somme

Chapter Six
45
Vimy Ridge

Chapter Seven
51
Hill 70 and Lens

Chapter Eight
57
Passchendaele

Chapter Nine
65
The Battle of Amiens

Chapter Ten
70
Pursuit to Cambrai

Chapter Eleven
73
Cease-Fire

Epilogue
79

Questions
81

Glossary
85

Appendix A
88

Reference Notes
90

Suggested Reading
91

AUTHOR'S NOTE AND ACKNOWLEDGMENTS

This book is a fleeting glance at the Canadian Infantry in World War I. As it is written for the young, it does not dwell on the horrors of war which were an everyday occurrence during the four years of trench warfare. By the same token, it is not written with hopes of glorifying war. Only the men who fought it are worthy of glory.

Because this book deals only with the Canadian infantry units of 1914 - 1918, there are no references to the Royal Newfoundland Regiment. As Newfoundland did not enter Confederation until 1949, the Royal Newfoundland Regiment was not part of the Canadian Expeditionary Force. For those students interested in learning about the contributions and the sacrifices made by these island men in World War I, the book *The Fighting Newfoundlanders* by Colonel G.W.L. Nicholson C.D. is a must to read.

In compiling the facts, figures, and chronological order of this narrative I must acknowledge the superb Official History of the Canadian Army entitled *Canadian Expeditionary Force 1914-1919* by Colonel G.W.L. Nicholson, C.D. All casualty figures quoted by me were derived from his book.

Several of the veterans' quotations were taken from *The Suicide Battalion* (Hurtig, 1978) by McWilliams and Steel. An excellent collection of tape-recorded interviews which that book was based on is held at the Saskatchewan Archives Board in Regina.

I must also thank Mr. Tom Goulet for his support and undying enthusiasm.

If my father were still with me I would thank him for the maps and illustrations he produced.

Any errors which may occur in this text are the responsibility of me alone.

R.J.S., St. Catharines, Ontario, 1989

Map showing Sarajevo, the site in the Austro-Hungarian Empire of 1919, where the assassination of the Archduke Franz Ferdinand precipitated the First World War.

Chapter One

CANADA'S CALL TO ARMS

November 11, 1918, 9:55 a.m. "This morning at dawn Canadian troops of the First Army captured [the city of] Mons." Sixty-five minutes after that message was dispatched the Great World War came to an end. It would end with soldiers from Canada's 42 Battalion, Royal Highlanders of Canada, and Royal Canadian Regiment entering the very town where members of the old British Army first met the Germans in August 1914.

At the outbreak of the European war on 4 August 1914, the thought of a Canadian army division aiding England did not send shivers through the German high command. Nor did it send great sighs of relief through the British high command. In fact, the Canadians were looked upon as nothing more than undisciplined colonials who should be swallowed up as replacements in the British Army. How these undisciplined colonials became the storm troops and the elite of the Empire armies will be shown throughout this text.

On 28 June 1914 the Archduke, Franz Ferdinand, the heir to the Austro-Hungarian throne was assassinated. The murder took place in Sarajevo, the capital city of Bosnia, a Balkan province on the eastern shore of the Adriatic Sea.

Consequently, on 23 July 1914 Austria presented the Serbian government with a totally unrealistic ultimatum, knowing that Serbia could not possibly accept its terms. Aware that Russia was sympathetic toward Serbia, Austria obtained an assurance from Germany of German support should war with Serbia be necessary. Five days after the ultimatum was

Private Victor Ellis, 46th Battalion, with his kit issue.

delivered, and with no agreement reached with Serbia, Austria declared war on the Serbs.

Russia, slowly flexing its military muscles, began **mobilization** on 30 July. Germany protested the Russian mobilization and declared war on Russia on 1 August. Italy, the third member of the "Triple Alliance" (Germany, Austria, and Italy) reneged on its pledge of support and remained neutral until May 1915, when it entered the war on the allied side.

France and Russia had joined together in a defensive pact in 1894. In 1904 France and England had reached a military agreement, and a similar defensive pact had been reached between England and Russia in 1907. This became known as the "Triple Entente."

With Russia mobilizing, Germany sent a demand to France requesting France's intent. France replied that it "will act in accordance with her interests."[1] On 3 August Germany declared war on France.

Meanwhile, since the June assassination, England had been trying all avenues to preserve peace in Europe. All attempts had failed, but by 3 August England had still not made its intentions known. Germany then stated its desire to attack France through neutral Belgium.

On the morning of 4 August, elements of the German army marched into Belgium. By evening England, honouring an old treaty with Belgium, declared war on Germany. When England went to war, Canada went also.

How was it that Canada wound up in a European war by the stroke of a British parliamentary pen? It must be remembered that in 1914-Canada, Canada had virtually no parliamentary rights to forge its own foreign policy. Nor could the Canadian parliament have any part in the decision to make war or negotiate peace. In fact, it was not until 1931 with the signing of the Statute of Westminster that Canada could determine her own military destiny.

However, by 1914 Canada had at least obtained the right to call parliament in order to discuss the sending of an expeditionary force to Imperial defence abroad.[2] That Canada's sons would go to war was never in question. Only the size of the contingent was open for discussion.

At the outbreak of the war, Canada's small Permanent Force or Permanent Active Militia consisted of 3,110 all ranks and 684 horses.[3] However, for the previous three years, the

Sir Sam Hughes, Minister of Militia

bombastic Minister of Militia, Colonel (later the Honorary Lieutenant General, Sir) Sam Hughes had badgered his Prime Minister, Sir Robert Borden, and anyone else who would listen about an impending war with Germany. Hughes increased his department's spending by close to four million dollars during those three years, and the Non-Permanent Active Militia reached a strength of 74,213 all ranks plus 16,726 horses.

On receiving news of the war, Hughes immediately scrapped all the mobilization plans and, instead, sent out 226 night telegrams directly to the local unit commanders in the Active Militia directing them to remit "rolls containing the names of volunteers willing to go overseas."[4]

Sir Robert Borden, Prime Minister of Canada during the First World War.

    This, of course, was the cause of much confusion and exasperation in the civil and military hierarchy. Regardless, Hughes forged ahead and, much to the surprise of everyone but himself, assembled 33,000 troops at the newly erected camp at Valcartier, Quebec, by 8 September 1914.
    Training and outfitting of the new **battalions** began in earnest. Already a privately formed Canadian unit, the Princess Patricia's Canadian Light Infantry, had embarked for overseas. This battalion would stay with a British brigade until joining the 3rd Canadian Division in 1915.
    The young recruits at Valcartier were eager for what they saw as a great adventure, so they were quick to please their

training officers. So adept were they that by the end of September the 1st Canadian Division were on their way to Quebec City, where they would board the transport ships that would take them to Southampton, England.

The infantry, armed with their Canadian-made Ross rifles, the artillery with their guns, **gun carriages**, and horses, and the cavalry units with their mounts all flooded to the docks. By the evening of 1 October, "thirty loaded transports had moved out into the St. Lawrence [River]."[5] The ships then gathered in the Gaspé to await their Royal Navy escorts. On the afternoon of 3 October the convoy weighed anchor and proceeded to the open sea.

After a quiet twelve-day crossing of the Atlantic Ocean, a last minute enemy submarine scare sent the ships to the port of Plymouth, England.

Confusion reigned supreme on the Plymouth docks, and it was nine days before the last units were able to leave their ship. From Plymouth the men departed by train and began their journey to their camp on Salisbury Plain.

At this camp began sixteen weeks of intense training. The ***division*** was spread out over four different camp sights in the area. Some units were lucky enough to have wooden huts to live in, while others had to make do with canvas tents. All men agreed on two characteristics of their stay on the plain — rain and mud. This was but a hint of what would greet them in France.

With weather conditions steadily deteriorating, a proper training agenda was next to impossible to keep. But the weather could not dampen the spirit of the men, and they pressed on eagerly with their training. Much to everyone's surprise, there was even a bit of discipline showing through while on parade and on leave. From a ragtag division of colonials there appeared, after sixteen weeks, a body of men that would match almost any in the British regular army. No one could deny that they lacked a little polish or that perhaps they were still a little too freewilled, but this independence was the very thing that by 1918 would make them just a little better than the rest.

Chapter Two

BAPTISM OF FIRE

By the time the 1st Canadian Division arrived in France, the invading German Army had been fought to a standstill. From the unsuccessful outflanking movements by the belligerent armies in 1914, there now was established an almost continuous line of opposing trenches, stretching from the Swiss border in the south to the north sea on the Belgian coast. It was into one small section of these trenches that the men from Canada entered.

An officer from the 2nd Canadian Battalion later recalled, "They entered a short stretch of trench, a narrow, dark canyon, with damp walls built up, for the most part, with sandbags. The **star shells** made strange shadows on the side of the trench; and the eeriness of the situation was intensified by the vicious crack or zip of bullets above them."[1]

The "zip" of bullets would soon be a common sound to these young Canadian volunteers. Within two months they would find themselves not only under rifle and artillery fire, but also meeting the enemy as they choked from the poison gas that the Germans had unleashed.

When the 1st Division moved into Belgium in April 1915, they thought of themselves as hardened veterans. After all, hadn't they completed several trench tours? And they had actually assisted, albeit in a small manner, the allied attack on Neuve Chapelle in March. Regardless of how the Canadians felt, the British high command was still somewhat skeptical of their fighting ability. The 22 April 1915 would change

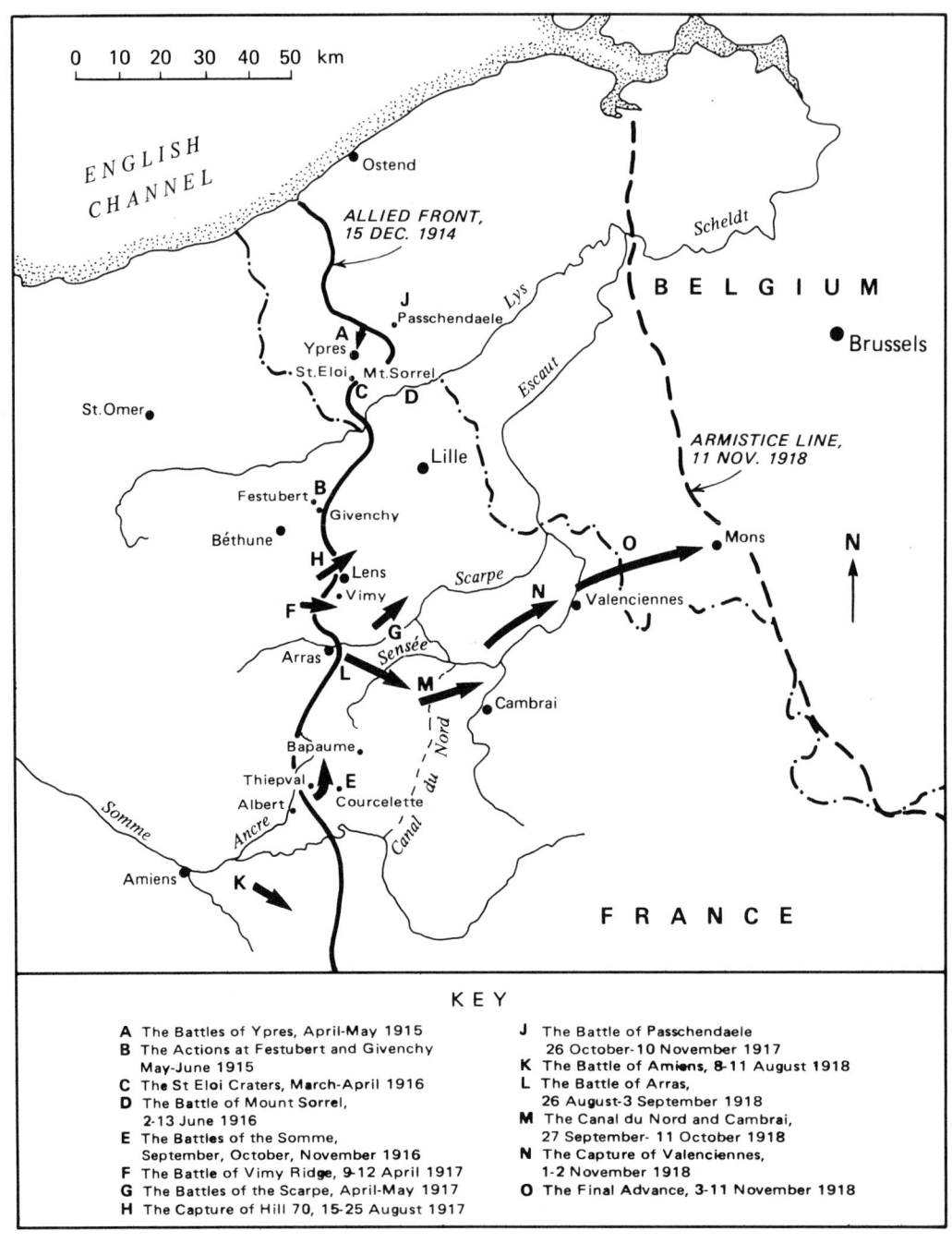

THE WESTERN FRONT, 1914 - 1918
Canadian Operations

forever the British opinion of these rowdy Canadian lads.

That particular day found the men of the 1st Canadian Division in trenches in the already infamous Ypres Salient. The salient was a "bulge" into the enemy line which was created in October 1914, when the British and Indian armies had successfully kept the Germans from capturing the city of Ypres.

During the late afternoon of the twenty-second, the Germans released chlorine gas from their front-line trenches. When released from the steel bottles the gas formed a yellowish-green cloud and, carried by a light breeze, rolled across **no-man's-land** and into the trenches of a French Territorial Division on the Canadians' left flank. These bewildered men from Africa panicked and ran away from the gas leaving a great gap next to the Canadians.

Without hesitation the Canadians dropped their left flank back and began moving into the gap. All the while, they were under tremendous shell and rifle fire and were also being choked by the gas. Then the Germans, wearing gauze masks, appeared like ghosts from behind the gas cloud.

Contact was soon lost between the battalions and their brigade headquarters. Because of the heavy shelling, gas, and general confusion on the battlefield, the brigade headquarters lost contact with 1st Divisional Headquarters which was situated near the village of Brielen, about eight kilometres west of the front line. With little or no communication between these headquarters, the fighting soon became a battle handled by **N.C.O.'s**, privates, and platoon officers. Germans were getting behind some of the isolated Canadians and firing into them from the rear. Coughing and gasping for breath, their eyes nearly blinded from the gas, the young rookies held on to their positions and effectively slowed the enemy's advance.

The 13th Battalion, Royal Highlanders of Canada, "Inspired by the gallant leadership . . . fought a dauntless fight . . . . But even sublime courage can not withstand fire and steel. Overwhelmed at last . . . their men as has not been killed were . . . surrounded and captured."[2]

So desperate was the fighting that in some areas it was a wild melee. To make matters worse for the Canadians,

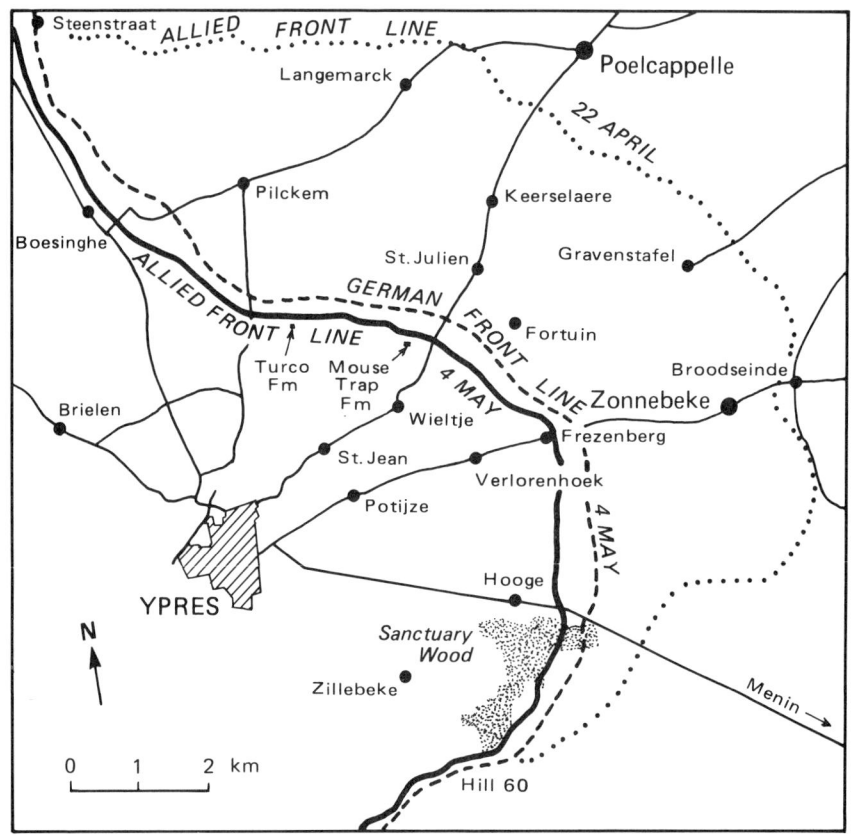

THE YPRES SALIENT, 22 April - 4 May 1915
Site of first German poison gas attack.

their rifle bolts began to jam. Men were seen in tears as they hammered on the bolts with their spades or boot heels. The Canadian-made Ross rifle had let the soldiers down in their hour of need.

Those who were able to find an abandoned British Lee-Enfield rifle threw their Ross away and carried on with the other weapon. Others found German Mauser rifles and used them. Others fought on with just their bare hands.

The situation by late evening was critical, but the German advance seemed to have ceased for the day. British and Canadian reserve troops began coming up to support the front-

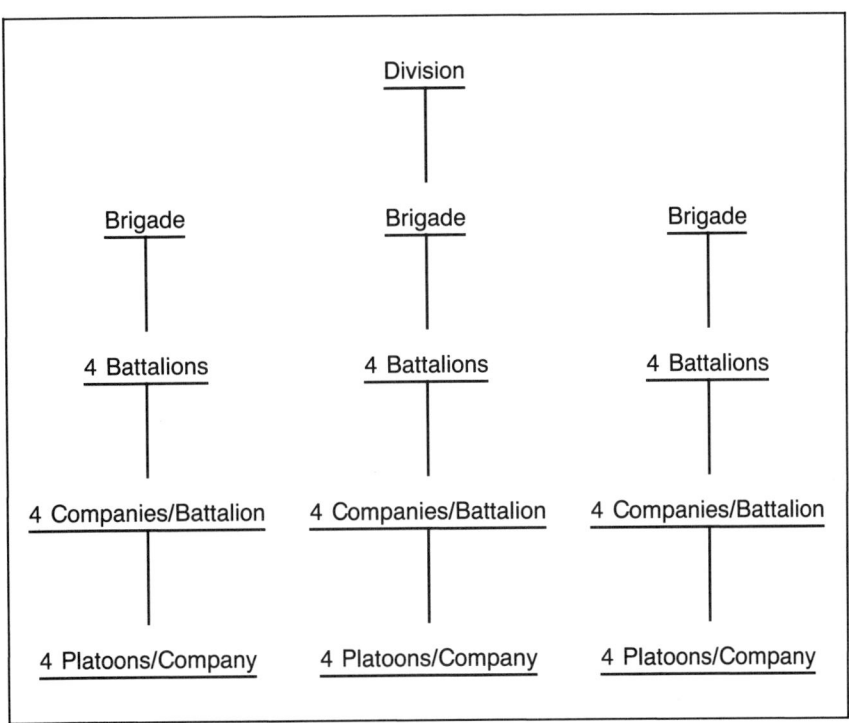

DIVISIONAL HIERARCHY

line units. Gas still clung to the ground and gathered in shell holes. Khaki-clad figures, their faces masked in water or urine-soaked kerchiefs, made their way forward and tried to establish an unbroken line.

By morning it was clear that if it had not been for the gallant action of the young Canadians the city of Ypres would have fallen to the enemy.

The Second Battle of Ypres, by which it became known, was to rage into May with more poison gas attacks and much more hand-to-hand fighting. The Canadian division was finally withdrawn from the battle zone on 4 May 1915.

On 8 May 1915, as the 1st Division was trying to reorganize in *reserves,* their brothers in the Princess Patricia's Canadian Light Infantry began to play their part in the Ypres battles. In a last attempt to push into the city of Ypres, the Germans launched another attack on the Frezenberg Ridge. Here the

"Pats" were blown out of their trenches by shellfire and had to seek shelter in shell holes behind their front line. Though battered and their numbers depleted, the surviving "Pats" kept up a rapid fire on the advancing enemy and were able to slow the advance. It is of major importance to note that the Princess Patricia's were armed with the Lee-Enfield rifle. It did not fail them. When the "Pats" were relieved that night by the 3rd Battalion, King's Royal Rifles, their total trench strength was four officers and one hundred and fifty men. The day's casualties* totalled 392, all ranks.3

The Second Battle of Ypres was indeed the Canadians' baptism of fire. The 1st Division and the Princess Patricia's Canadian Light Infantry had suffered a combined casualty list of 6,714 men. Their reputation as fierce fighting men was well earned during the fighting of April and May 1915. The three Canadian divisions which were to follow in 1915 and 1916 would enhance that reputation.

*NOTE: Unless otherwise stated, casualty figures are a total of those killed and wounded.

Chapter Three

CANADA CARRIES ON
May - December 1915

The 1st Canadian Division was not long in reserves when they heard heavy gunfire to the south. The French had begun their May offensive against the enemy on the heights of Vimy Ridge. The British, providing a diversion for the French, launched an attack against Aubers Ridge and the village of Festubert.

At Aubers Ridge the British attack was a complete failure. No ground was gained at a cost of 11,000 casualties. Incredibly, the attack on Festubert was still carried on, but soon bogged down. By 18 May it was decided that the Canadians should be pulled out of reserves to carry on with the Festubert battle.

In the two following attacks, men from the 2nd and 3rd Brigades flung themselves across water-logged fields only to be cut down by withering machine gunfire. However, on 20 May attacking parties from the 16th Battalion, Canadian Scottish, fought their way into an orchard and dug in 100 metres short of the German trench. A few days later the Canadians were relieved and returned to their rest **billets.** For their efforts in gaining approximately 500 metres of shell-swept mud they suffered 2,468 casualties.

Less than a month would pass before men from the 1st and 2nd Battalions would find themselves thrown into the fighting near the town of Givenchy. But now they would be going into battle armed with the Lee-Enfield rifle, as the Canadian-made Ross rifle had proven to be untrustworthy and

Site of the attack by the 16th Battalion, Canadian Scottish, on the orchard, May 1915.

had been withdrawn from the 1st Division.

At fifteen minutes before the zero hour of 5:45 p.m. on 16 June, two artillery pieces that had been concealed in the front-line trench opened fire on the enemy's line and blasted an opening through the barbed wire. The enemy quickly retaliated by dropping a **barrage** of shells on the assembled Canadians, inflicting heavy casualties.

At zero hour, a mine* was exploded under the enemy trench, but a miscalculation of the amount of explosives caused severe damage to the Canadian line. Even in the ensuing chaos, the Canadians leapt out of their trenches and stormed the German line.

The 1st Battalion's **bombers** reached the German support

*NOTE: See illustration p. 23.

```
                    ENEMY STRONG POINT
ALLIED TRENCH           AND TRENCH
         BARBED WIRE
         "NO-MAN'S-LAND"...

     Approximately 15 metres

     TUNNEL  1.5 to 2 metres in diameter
              BACK FILL – PRIOR
              TO DETONATING

                        HIGH
                        EXPLOSIVES
NOT TO SCALE
```

Cutaway of simplified mining operation.

line and attempted to bomb left and right along the trench. But a shortage of hand bombs and a fierce enemy counterattack forced them back into the German's first line.

The 2nd Battalion, with two supporting **platoons** from the 3rd Battalion, Toronto Regiment, were fighting in and around the newly-blown mine crater. They too soon ran low on bombs and ammunition. A reinforcing **company** from the 3rd Battalion attempted to push foward, but was caught in the trenches by intense enemy fire. By 10 a.m. a withdrawal was ordered.

A new attack on the enemy stronghold, known as the Duck's Bill, was ordered for 4.45 p.m. The 3rd Battalion was to have the dubious honour of leading the attack. Captain Richardson of the 2nd Battalion later recalled, "The attack seemed . . . futile and hopeless . . . The attackers had no supporting fire . . . . They were mostly shot down as they climbed over the **parapet**."[1] Mercifully, the attack was called off. The net result for the fighting was no ground gained at a cost of 500 casualties to the three battalions involved.

The division was pulled out of that sector on 24 June and moved north to the Ploegstraat (soon to be known as Plugstreet by the soldiers) area. It was now that a three-month lull in the fighting seemed to settle over the western front. However, a lull in the fighting did not mean a restful period for the infantrymen.

"The order of the day — and night — was dig! The demands in the way of new trenches were insatiable. The men learned how to fight a war of shovels and sandbags."[2]

Almost every night, wiring parties would slip out into no-man's-land with their bundles of barbed wire and wooden stakes. While some of the men would pound the stakes or wooden crosspieces into the ground, others would string the barbed wire between them. Of course, all this work was being carried on within hearing distance of the enemy, who would soon send up flares and traverse the area with machine gunfire.

When a flare went up the men would have to freeze in their positions. Strange as it might seem, if they didn't move they couldn't be spotted in the ghostly white light. When the flare had sputtered out, no-man's-land would come alive again to the sounds of muffled hammer blows and the 'ping' of barbed wire.

After perhaps three or four hours of this type of work, the exhausted working parties would return to their billets for the day, only to be called on again the following evening for another night of hard and dangerous labour.

While doing their tour of trench duty in the Ploegstraat sector, the men not on sentry watch would spend a great deal of time repairing the **breastworks** of the trench. Because of the high water table in the area, these trenches were rather shallow and had to be built up into sandbagged breastworks. Enemy shellfire was continually blowing gaps in the walls, and an enemy sniper would quickly site in on these spots, waiting to shoot an unwitting soldier as he passed in front of the gap.

By September the 2nd Canadian Division had joined their brothers in the trenches. They too were soon involved in the tedious work of keeping their trenches in repair. During the dry months this work proved trying enough; October and November

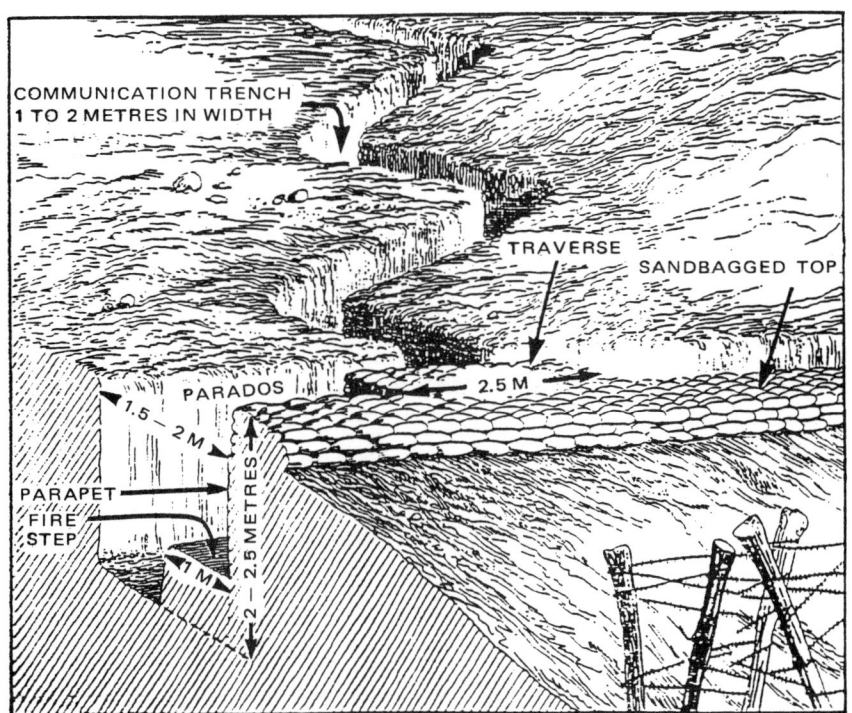
A typical front-line and communication trench.

proved to be absolutely horrible.

Torrential rains throughout October and November turned the battlefields into virtual swamps. Shell holes quickly filled with water and slopped over into other holes, creating almost lake-like conditions. Sandbags literally seemed to dissolve, and great lengths of the Canadians' trenches and breastworks seemed to melt away. Trenches filled with water, and men had to stand thigh deep in the cold, muddy slop. The Germans, always on the higher ground, made great sport of draining their trenches into the Canadian lines.

Many Canadians were killed or wounded as they tried to crawl over the back of the trench to get some relief from the wet. The enemy snipers, never missing an opportunity, would calmly pick the men off as they struggled out of the slime.

There was no escape from the wretched mess of the front line. Even the trench shelters or **dugouts** collapsed, leaving the men to huddle, haunches in the water and ground sheets wrapped about their shoulders and waiting for some kind of change. The change that came was not one of rest and relaxation, but one that was supposed to instill a new spirit for the offensive. The Canadians were about to be introduced to the trench raid.

In brief, a raid would be preceded by a quick artillery bombardment on a selected section of the enemy trench, quickly followed by the raiding party dashing across no-man's-land and into the bombarded section of the enemy trench. Here the party was to secure prisoners for identification, destroy dugouts and stores, then immediately return to their own lines. This type of action, it was assured, would keep the enemy nervous and lower morale.

The first raid* staged by the Canadian divisions took place on the night of the 16/17 November 1915. Volunteers from the 7th Battalion and the 5th Battalion were to make a two-pronged attack on a stronghold in front of the village of Messines known as La Petite Douve Farm. The 7th was to attack just south of the farm and enter a strongly fortified section of trench, while the 5th was to perform a diversionary attack against an area three hundred and fifty metres southeast of the 7th's objective.

On the morning of the sixteenth the artillery opened fire on the enemy barbed wire and later began a bombardment on the farm. That night, while the raiders waited in their trenches, two parties crept out into no-man's-land. One group carried small portable bridges which they laid across the tiny Douve River. The second party crawled up to the barbed wire and cut the entanglements that the artillery had missed. By 2.30 a.m. the raiding party, their faces covered with black crepe masks and all forms of identification removed, were ready to go over the top.

At a prearranged signal, both parties began to cross the muddy stretch between the lines. On the right the 5th Battalion immediately ran into a snag. A ditch they had to cross was flooded and concealed rolls of barbed wire that the enemy had

---

*NOTE: The first Canadians involved in a raid were from the Princess Patricia's Canadian Light Infantry. This took place on 28 February 1915.

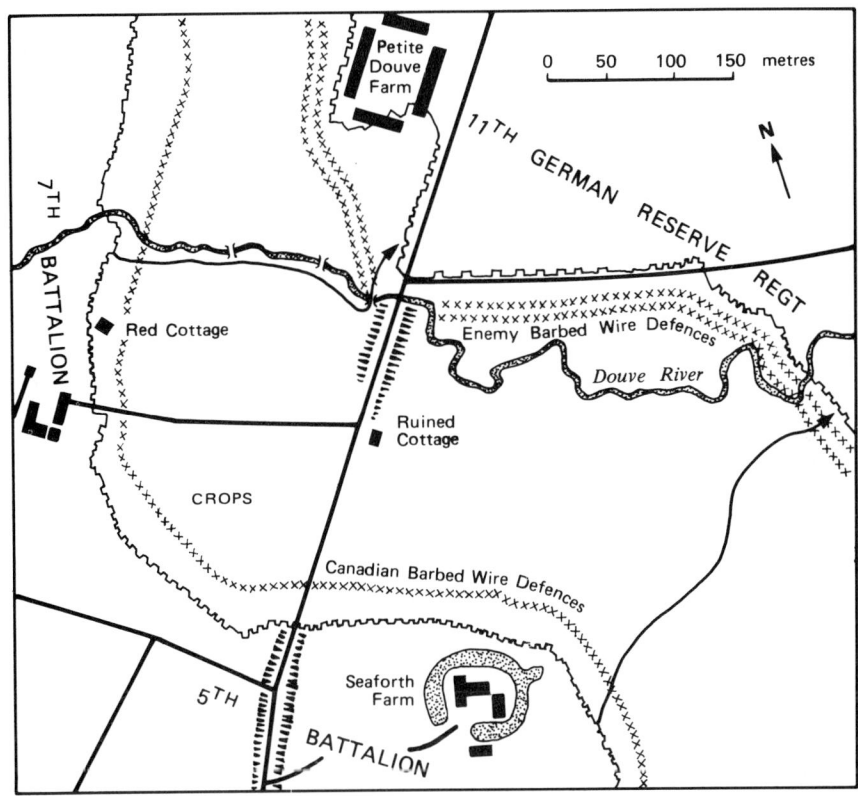

First Canadian Corps trench raid, 16 - 17 November 1915.

hidden in it. A few men became tangled in this wire and their struggles to get out alerted the German sentries.

The enemy opened a hot and heavy fire to which the Canadians cooly replied with a deluge of hand grenades. The raiders from the 5th Battalion quickly realized that it would be futile to carry on with their raid. Luckily, the men caught in the wire were able to get free, and they all safely returned to their trenches.

The 7th Battalion to the north were enjoying what would later be called a model raid. They crossed the portable bridges, dashed through the cut wire and stormed the enemy's trenches. The Germans here had been caught totally off guard and the captain of the raiding party "jumped clean upon the German sentry sheltering beneath a sheet of corrugated iron, which went down clattering."3

Wiring parties dashed left and right and threw wire entanglements into the trench to prevent counterattacks from the flanks. Riflemen and bombers created havoc, as they ran along the trench shooting and bombing at every traverse* and lobbing grenades down into the dugouts. To add to the din, the Canadian artillery began a bombardment on the enemy's support lines and communication trenches. This they hoped would catch any German reinforcements as they tried to come forward.

In twenty minutes the Canadians were on their way back. Before them hustled twelve bewildered prisoners, while in their wake remained at least thirty killed and wounded Germans. An unknown amount of dugouts had been blasted and the trench was in ruins. The raiders suffered two casualties.

These two raids were just the beginning of what would become a Canadian trademark. From the 16/17 November 1915 until the end of the war, it was very rare if some Canadian battalion were not raiding the enemy's line.

As the war dragged on, these raids became even more enterprising and some took on the appearance of a full scale offensive. German prisoners readily admitted that they hated to see the Canadians in the lines opposite them, as they knew that some night these brash young men would come hurtling into their trenches.

Nineteen fifteen was drawing to a close and the newly-formed Canadian Corps, like most of their British counterparts, were left wallowing in the cold mud. A new malady dubbed "trench feet" soon became almost epidemic. Because of the constant immersion of the feet in the cold and somewhat septic water, they would swell and slowly blacken as gangrene set in. Orders were issued to those going into the front line that "boots and **puttees** will be removed at least once in every 24 hours. Feet and legs will be dried, rubbed and greased [with whale oil] and dry socks put on."4 Only the daily issue of half a **gill** of rum seemed to bring any comfort to the front-line troops.

Such was the lot of the Canadian infantryman on the western front as 1915 drew to a close.

*NOTE: See illustration p. 25.

Chapter Four

HOLDING THE LINE

By the end of December 1915, the Canadian Corps had been joined by the 3rd Canadian Division. And in January 1916, the 3rd was being rotated into the relief system with the 1st and 2nd Divisions.

The area of Canadian responsibility was now extended to cover a nine kilometre front starting just below the Ypres Salient. Here they would remain for three months battling the cold, the mud, the lice, and the enemy. A routine which consisted of constant patrolling and raiding was carried out until April 1916, when the 2nd Division was called on to relieve the exhausted British troops in front of the town of St. Eloi.

On 27 March, six British mines were blown to eliminate a German salient at St. Eloi. The ensuing battle for these craters turned into a confusing slugfest fought in swamp-like conditions. By 4 April the British battalions were spent and the Canadians were ordered to relieve the decimated British units.

The first two days in the St. Eloi sector found the Canadians employed in trying to strengthen their almost impossible positions. The newly captured water-filled trenches and craters still held wounded British and German soldiers who could not be taken out of the lines. Bodies of the dead were scattered everywhere and had to be unceremoniously dealt with. The weather conditions were terrible, and the unrelenting enemy fire soon weakened the Canadians.

At 3.30 a.m. on 6 April the Germans launched an attack

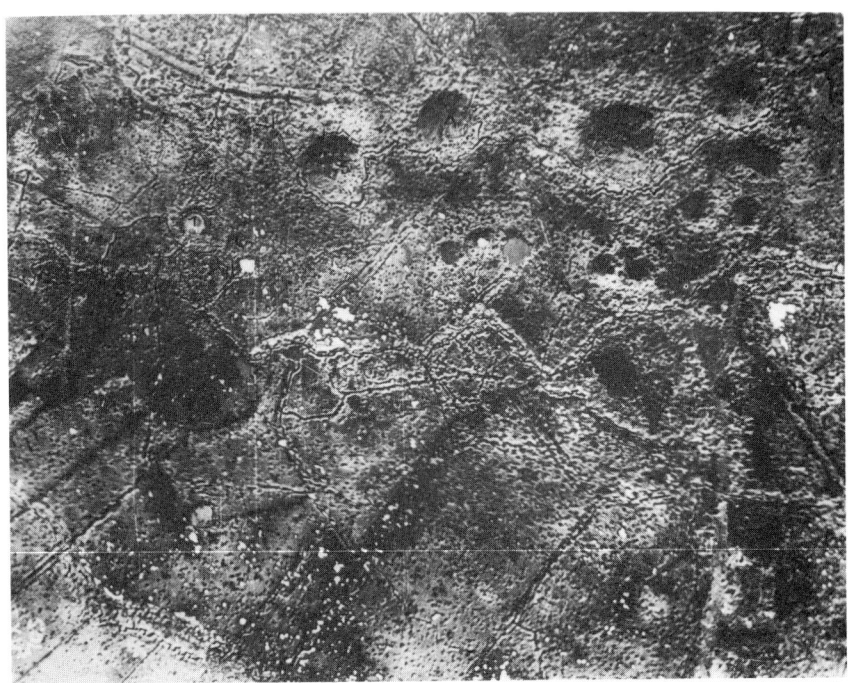

St. Eloi craters. Note the shell-blasted battleground. Enemy trenches appear in central part of photo.

on the Canadians who were in the midst of an inter-battalion relief. The surprise was total and the Germans swept into the Canadian lines.

Though fighting valiantly, the exhausted Canadians were soon driven out of craters 2, 3, 4, and 5. Bombers from the 27th and 29th Battalions were unable to get near craters 2 and 3. Parties from the 31st and 28th Battalions became confused in the wasteland and consolidated craters 5 and 6, but reported that they had recaptured numbers 4 and 5.

This state of confusion lasted until 16 April, when it was finally realized that there had been a gross error in the reporting of the capture of craters 4 and 5. By 19 April the sledgehammer blows from both sides petered out and St. Eloi became another desolate, static position. The 2nd Canadian Division had suffered 1,373 casualties.

Members of the 2nd Canadian Division in the line near the St. Eloi Craters. Note steel helmets which were issued to the troops in April 1916, prior to taking over the British positions in front of the craters. Because of a supply problem, only fifty helmets were issued per company.

The 1st Canadian Division had been bloodied at Ypres in 1915; the 2nd Division was now licking its wounds in front of St. Eloi; the 3rd Division had by now become trench-wise and held an area of the Ypres Salient from Hill 60, over Mount Sorrel, Hill 61, and Hill 62. On 2 June 1916 the 3rd Division would receive its baptism of fire.

At 6 a.m. on 2 June, a tornado of steel fell on the 8th and 7th Brigades between Mount Sorrel and Sanctuary Wood located on the southwest side of the Ypres Salient. The Canadian lines were pounded for four hours. Then, at 1 p.m. four enemy mines were blown in front of the Mount Sorrel trenches. With the blowing of the mines, the Germans attacked. If they could capture Mount Sorrel and Hill 62, they could possibly turn

Holding The Line 33

Dugouts in the Ypres Salient, July 1916.

the allied flank and push into Ypres. And, if Ypres could be captured, the gateway to the channel ports would be opened.

The Germans met with very little opposition from the pulverized Canadian trenches, and it was only the 5th Canadian Mounted Rifles stationed behind the decimated front-line units who were able to stop the flood of Germans on Maple Copse.

The "Princess Pats", now with the 3rd Canadian Division and on the right of the 1st Canadian Mounted Rifles, held on to their sector for eighteen hours and kept the enemy in check. In doing so, they suffered almost 400 casualties.

Quick Canadian counterattacks steadied the line, and preparations were begun in earnest for a major assault to retake the lost ground.

On 12 June, the German positions came under a crushing ten-hour allied artillery barrage. At 1:30 a.m. on the thirteenth

◄ *In the trenches, early July 1916. Note the Canadian-made Ross Rifles.*

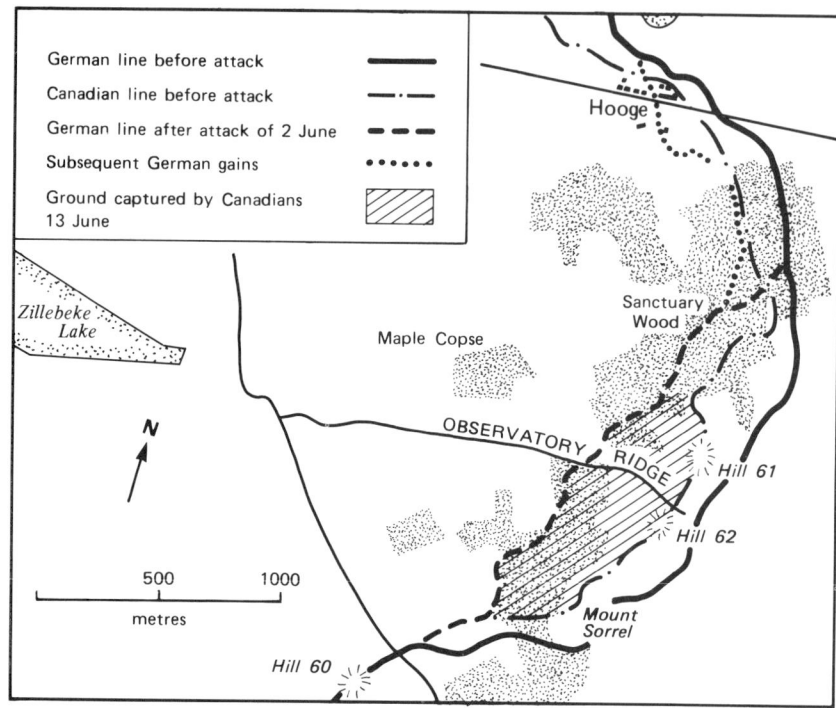

MOUNT SORREL, JUNE 1916

fresh troops from the 1st Division charged into the enemy's line. It was a perfectly planned attack and went off like clockwork. Within hours nearly all of their old positions were recaptured, and the enemy was driven back to its lines of two weeks previous. During this approximate two weeks of fighting, the Canadians had suffered about 8,000 casualties.

Meanwhile, further south on the rolling Picardy plains of France, a new British offensive was about to be launched. This offensive would become known as the Battle of the Somme and would rage from July until the end of November 1916.

Division after division and corps after corps of the British Army were poured into the slaughter. Troops from Australia, New Zealand, and South Africa were thrown against the mighty Somme defences and died there. By late August the British high command needed fresh troops to continue the battle. Once again, the Canadians, now with the addition of a 4th Division, were called upon to do battle.

Chapter Five

THE BATTLE OF THE SOMME

September 1916 found the 1st, 2nd, and 3rd Divisions on the move south to the Somme battlefields. The recently arrived 4th Division would remain in the Ypres Salient to receive its trench indoctrination and would not head to the Somme area until October.

What was to become the "Big Push" of the war became a battle of attrition. Attrition can best be described as follows: if Canada had 100,000 men and lost 99,000, and the enemy had 90,000 men and lost all 90,000, Canada would be the winner with 1,000 men remaining. This way of waging war gained prominence in 1916 with the Battle of the Somme and the Battle of Verdun. It reached its peak in 1917 in the waterlogged battlefields before the village of Passchendaele in the Ypres Salient.

The 1st Division took over trenches from just east of the now pulverized town of Pozières, along 2,743 metres of battered trenches to just west of a German stronghold known as Mouquet Farm. During the three days that the 3rd Brigade held this section, they suffered nearly 1,000 casualties.

The Canadian participation in the Somme battles can be broken into three phases: 1. Flers-Courcelette; 2. Thiepval Ridge; 3. The Battle of the Ancre Heights.

The first phase began at 6.20 a.m. on 15 September 1916 with the 2nd Division on a two-brigade front attacking toward the town of Courcelette. The two brigades were to attack astride the Albert-Bapaume Road and capture the defenses in front

The sugar refinery near Courcelette, on the Somme.

of the town, Candy Trench, a section of Sugar Trench, and the strongly defended sugar factory before Courcelette. A brigade from the 3rd Division was to provide covering fire for the 2nd's left flank.

Two new innovations were to be used in this battle. One was the creeping barrage behind which the infantry would slowly follow. In theory, this rolling wall of artillery fire would wipe out anything in front of the advancing infantry. All that would be left for the "foot sloggers" to do would be the **mopping up** of prisoners.

The second innovation was the introduction of tanks. For more than two years of attack and counterattack barbed wire and machine gunfire had stopped any significant gains. Now, these heavily armoured, caterpillar-tracked vehicles, bristling with machine guns or canon, should be able to trundle through the barbed wire and take out the enemy machine gun nests with ease. Again, in theory, the infantry man would just walk along after the tanks and occupy the enemy's trench.

On the night of 14/15 September Sergeant John Armstrong of the 3rd Battery Canadian Field Artillery was sitting by his artillery piece chatting with his crew when they heard a strange racket on the road behind them. "It was a moonlit night and we wondered what kind of monsters they were. They [the tanks] were going up the road between Ovillers and Pozières and you could hear them coming for miles. They made an awful row as they went by our battery."[1] The tanks were rolling into position.

Promptly at 6.20 a.m. the barrage thundered and the Canadians moved forward. Of the six tanks allotted to the Canadian front, only one achieved its objective. Four were knocked out by shellfire and the fifth had broken down before it crossed the start line. However, the infantrymen pressed on and by 7.30 a.m. both brigades reported their objectives taken.

In the meantime, the brigade supporting the 2nd Division on the left stormed into and captured a section of the Mouquet Farm redoubt and part of the Fabeck Graben trench system. This trench system ran up the gentle slope from Mouquet Farm to the village of Courcelette. By 11 a.m. it was decided that the Canadians should continue on and capture the entire village and the remainder of the Fabeck Graben Trench.

In late afternoon and in broad daylight, battalions from the 5th, 7th, and 8th brigades went over the top. The Courcelette defenders offered stiff resistance for fifteen minutes, but the 25th and the 22nd Battalions swept them aside and pushed on through the village. The mopping up was left to the 26th New Brunswick Battalion and it represented the most difficult task of the attack on the village.

Germans, who had taken refuge in their well-camouflaged dugouts, began slipping out and engaging the 26th, who were supposed to be entering a cleared objective. This winkling out of the enemy would take two days before Courcelette was finally cleared. The 26th suffered 224 casualties for their efforts.

Meanwhile, on the left, while the 42nd Battalion and the Princess Pats were battling their way into the remainder of Fabeck Graben, the 4th Canadian Mounted Rifles ran into

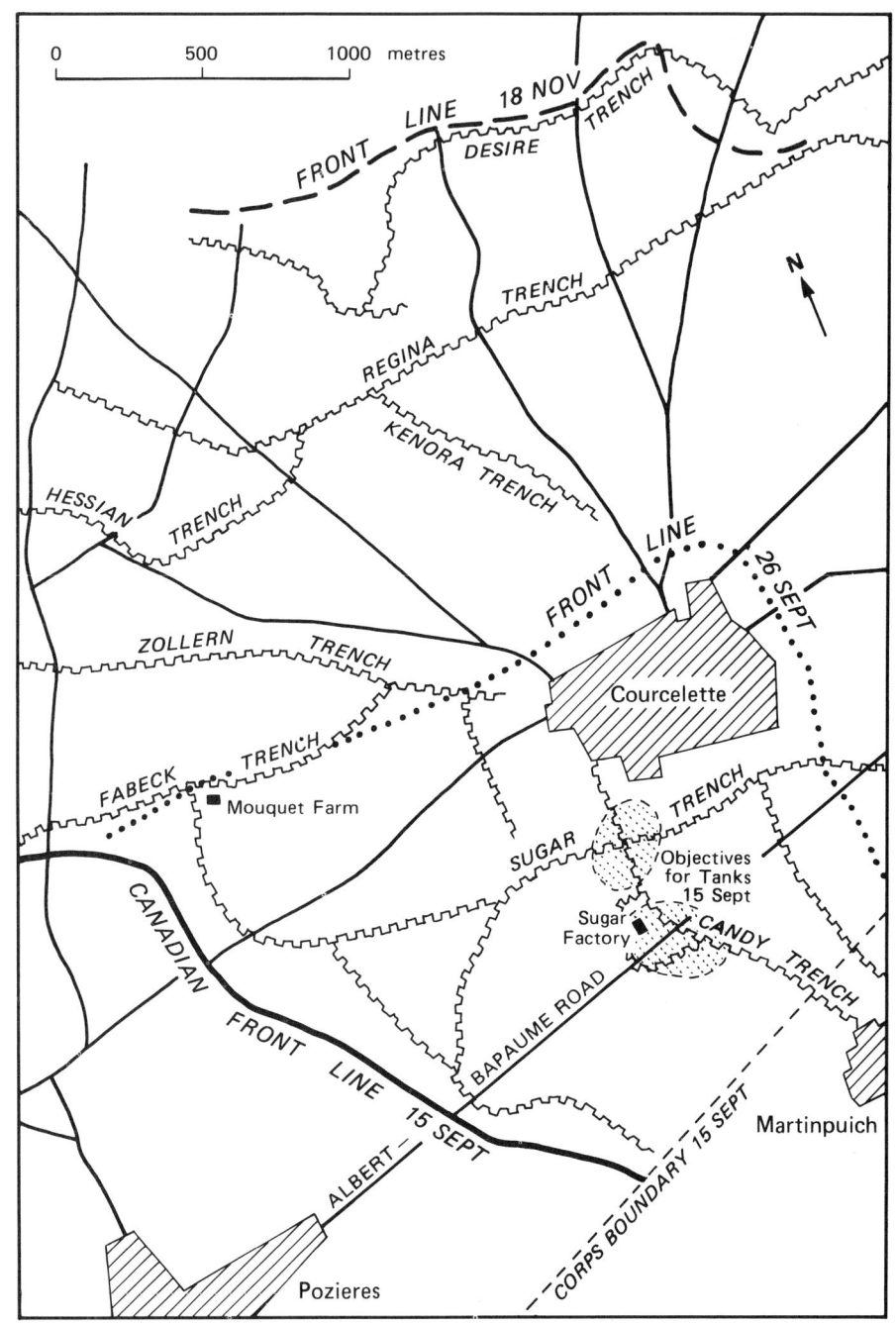

SOMME, 1916

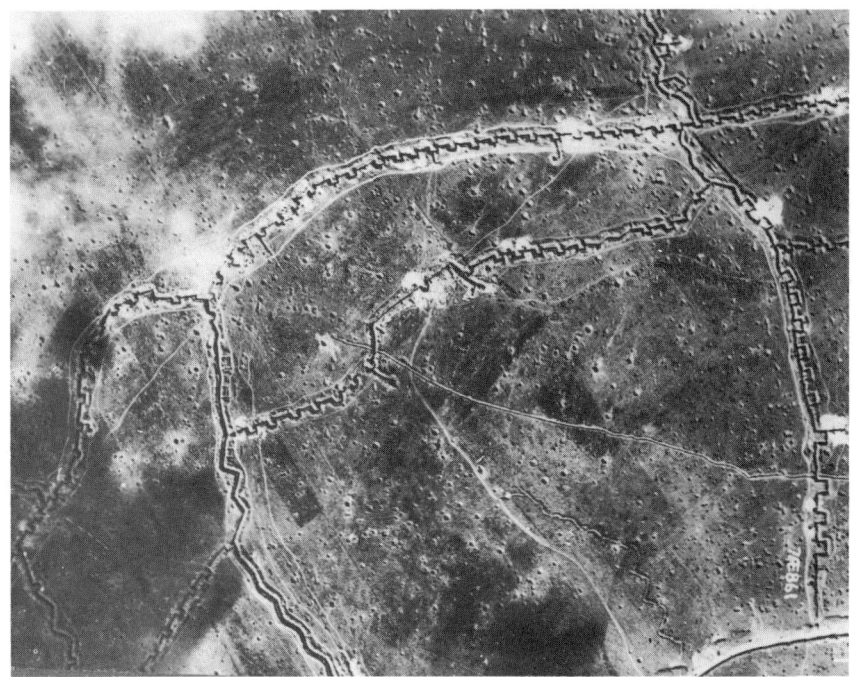

Part of the Hessian Trench system on the Somme. Note the traverses in the trench lines.

serious problems. They had not received any orders until the last moment and had no plan of attack. "C" Company were late to the attack and had to come overland to their starting positions. In doing so, almost two platoons were completely wiped out by enemy machine gunfire. "B" Company, assaulting on their own, were able to overcome the tenacious enemy and gain their objectives.

This effectively ended the first phase, though the Canadians came under constant shellfire and enemy counterattacks over the next few days. The week of fighting around Courcelette and the Fabeck Graben Trench system had resulted in the Canadians suffering almost 7,300 casualties.

Phase two was to begin on 26 September with attacks on a one thousand metre frontage east of Courcelette. The objectives were to be Hessian Trench, Kenora Trench, and Regina Trench.

On the right of Courcelette the attack went well and most objectives were taken. However, the 3rd Brigade in the centre ran into tremendous artillery and machine gunfire. Those that were able to make their objectives came under severe fire from the flanks and had to withdraw to safer positions. On the left, elements of the 2nd Brigade fought their way into Hessian Trench, but were not able to clear the entire trench of the enemy.

Attacks of this nature went on until 28 September as battalion after battalion was thrown against the German defences. By then, as one officer later reported, "The countryside is now one mass of shell holes everywhere you look. The woods are blown to pieces, and only a few branchless stumps remain . . . . As for towns and villages — well, they simply don't exist now."2

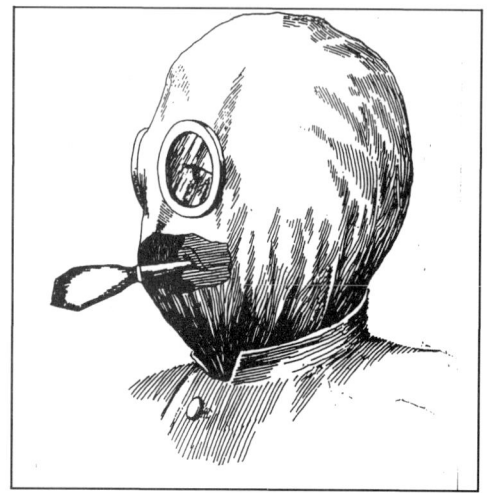

Illustration of a chemically treated gas helmet used by allies in 1916. A rubber-coated tube was held in the mouth, and, after inhaling air through the nose, the air was exhaled through the rubber tube. The tube was constructed in such a manner that it could not be used for inhaling.

By the end of the second phase the Canadians had cleared the heights of the Thiepval Ridge, but Regina Trench was still to be taken. Phase three, or The Battle of the Ancre Heights, was now about to begin. It would continue for six weeks, and the main objective would be the elusive Regina Trench.

The first two attacks on Regina Trench were put on by the first three divisions. The attack set for 1 October began in a drizzling rain and was a complete failure. Barbed wire, machine gunfire, and poor planning were enough to stop these gallant young Canadians.

The second attack took place on 8 October. Once again,

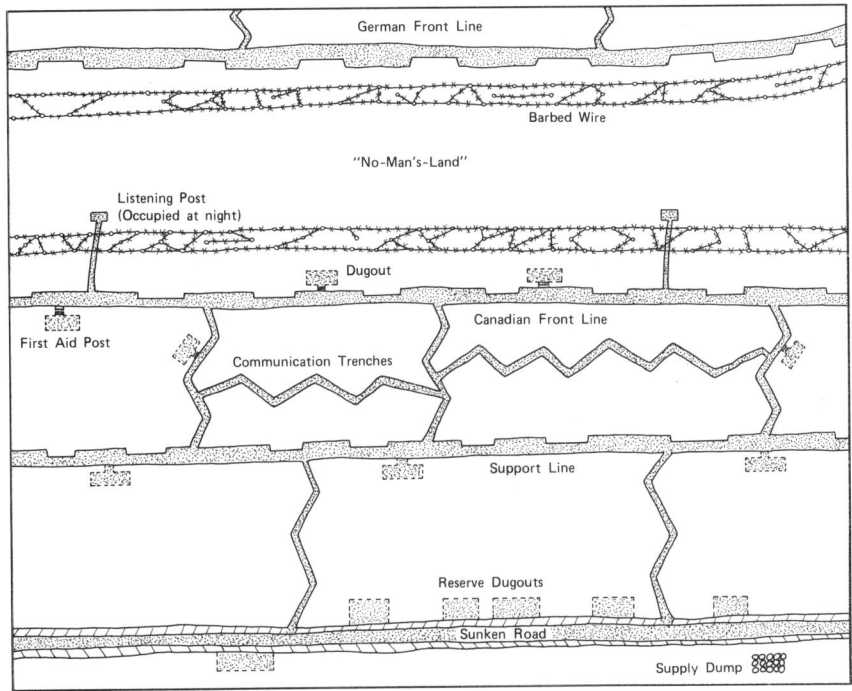

Overhead view of typical trench system.

the lack of any in-depth plan led the men into ever-present barbed wire and withering enemy fire. For this effort, 1,400 Canadians made the casualty lists.

Regina Trench was still intact, but the three Canadian divisions were exhausted. The 4th Division arrived on the Somme on 10 October and by the seventeenth they were on their own, as the other Canadian divisions had been withdrawn north to the Arras sector.

Not only would the 4th Division have to face the enemy on the Somme, they would also have to deal with the mud. Since the 4th's arrival, it had rained continuously, turning the battlefield, the support area, and the reserve area into a sea of mud. One private later recalled, "Our transport lines had weigh scales, and it was found that a man's clothing became so coated from half-frozen mud that together with his boots and puttees they weighed in the neighbourhood of 120 pounds

[54.4 kilograms], and in one case, 145 pounds [65.7 kilograms]."3

The men of the 4th Division were immediately put into the line. The two and one half months they had spent in the relatively quiet Ypres Salient had not prepared them for the horrors of what they would now encounter. A twenty year old sniper from the 46th Battalion later recalled, "I got my first glimpse of death . . . at Pozières. The dead had not been removed, and they were piled three deep . . . . Now we came to the trench [this was a **communication trench**] . . . God forbid anybody from seeing what I saw. Our barbed wire was fairly well intact, but it hung full of dead Canadians and Germans."4 This then was the Somme of October and November 1916.

An attack on 21 October was somewhat successful: 600 yards of Regina Trench fell to the men of the 11th Brigade. An attack on the remaining 640 metres of the trench was set for the twenty-fourth, but rain delayed it until the twenty-fifth.

The success of the twenty-first was not to be duplicated. A poor artillery barrage and murderous German machine gun-fire from the right sector cut great swaths through the attacking 44th Battalion. A supporting company from the 46th Battalion was also cut to pieces. The attack was a dismal failure. Accompanying this failure was a steady downpour. All operations came to a halt for the next two weeks.

On the night of 10/11 November the final attack on Regina Trench was launched. This time the artillery was more than successful. The enemy trench garrison had been almost wiped out to a man, and the cheering Canadians overran their objective. However, Regina Trench, which had cost the Canadians dearly, had been so pulverized that it was now virtually unfit for occupation or defence.

The final operation for the 4th Division on the Somme was an attack on Desire Trench which lay about 500 metres beyond Regina Trench. On 18 November the attack went in. On the left frontage, the 11th and 12th Brigades slogged their way through the mud and gained their objectives. On the right, the luckless 10th Brigade was again badly cut up. The 46th Battalion, thrown into battle for the third time in just over two

◀ *In the front-line trench, September 1916.*

weeks, was again cut to pieces and could not hold on to their slim gains. The 50th Battalion came under withering enemy fire from its flanks and had to withdraw to Regina Trench. By 8 p.m. the battle was called off. On the 19 November the torrential rains came again.

By the 28 November the 4th Division had been relieved, and, turning their backs on the Picardy battlefields, the depleted battalions began the march north to join the other three divisions. The two and one half months spent on the Somme cost the Canadian Corps 24,029 casualties.

Chapter Six

VIMY RIDGE

Seen at a distance from the west, Vimy Ridge appeared as a mist-shrouded rise that stretched along the Canadian front. From the south-east at Neuville St. Vaast, the Canadian sector of the ridge gently rose along a six kilometre front to the northwest where it was dissected by the small Souchez River. Just before this river valley the ridge was capped by a 120 metre knoll known as The Pimple. Across the river from The Pimple was the Notre Dame de Lorette Spur, where so many French died during their attack on the ridge in 1915.

If you climbed the ridge from the old Canadian lines and looked eastward over the crest towards the old German occupied territory, you would note its real defensive value. Spread out before and below you would be the entire Douai Plain and all its important coal mining centres. As long as Vimy Ridge remained in the enemy's hands, this prized territory would be safe from allied liberation.

If you then turned and looked westward from the crest of the ridge towards the old Canadian sector, a clear panorama of the entire Canadian front would lie before you. Roadways, communication trenches, supply dumps, and camps would come easily under German scrutiny and German artillery fire. It is a wonder that any troop movement could have been made during daylight hours without incurring the wrath of the enemy's artillery. It was, in front of this seemingly impregnable fortress of Vimy Ridge that the Canadians huddled down for the winter and spring of 1917.

When in late December of 1916 the Canadians arrived in front of the ridge, the area had become known as a quiet sector. The French in 1915 suffered 150,000 casualties trying to take the heights, and the British lost 50,000 in 1916. Since May 1916 a live-and-let-live attitude had been practiced by the belligerents on the slopes of the ridge. The battle-hardened Canadians would soon put an end to that.

On 20 December 400 raiders from the 1st Canadian Mounted Rifles stormed into the German lines and wreaked havoc, by destroying at least twenty-five dugouts and capturing nearly sixty prisoners.

Observation post near Vimy Ridge.

Smaller-sized raids were taking place at an average of one every three days, but, on 17 January 1917, 860 men from the 20th and 21st Battalions charged into the German trenches and for an hour ran amok, destroying all the dugouts in a 731 metre section. On 13 February almost 900 Canadians from the 10th Brigade surprised the now jittery enemy and inflicted about 160 casualties.

Luck had to change soon for these daring raiders and it did with a vengeance on the last night of February. A mass raid put on by 1700 volunteers from the 4th Division turned into a bloodbath, as the German artillery and riflemen caught the raiders in their own wire. Before the night was over, the raiders had suffered almost 700 casualties. That was to be the last of the big and elaborate raids to take place before the actual battle

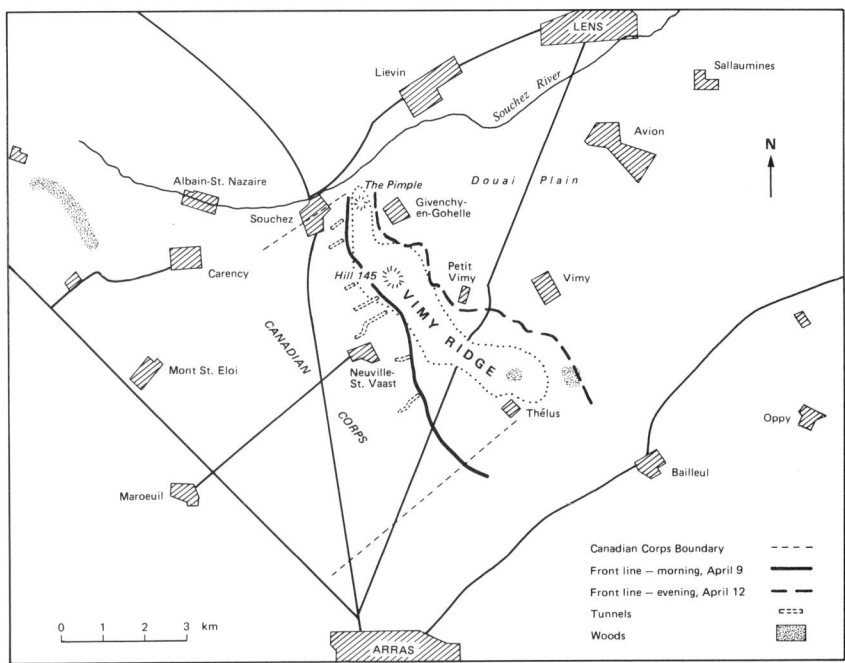

VIMY RIDGE, APRIL 1917

for Vimy Ridge began on 9 April 1917. However, from 20 March until the opening of the battle, the Canadians raided the Germans every night.

On the evening of 8 April the Canadian front was alive with khaki figures moving forward to their jumping-off positions. Almost as if by magic, the men began to disappear into the base of the ridge. During the months of occupation in front of the ridge, the engineers had dug great tunnels and galleries into the ridge. These tunnels led all the way from the rear to the front lines and, in many cases, out into mine craters in no-man's-land. By zero hour all the men would be safely hidden in their attack positions.

At 5.30 a.m. on 9 April, the rear of the Canadian lines exploded in a sheet of flames and a wall of noise, as almost 1,000 artillery pieces opened fire on the German lines. Seconds later the enemy's front lines disappeared in a cloud of smoke

Vimy Ridge. German prisoners being sent to the rear of the Canadian lines, 9 April 1917.

and flames, as the high explosives found their targets. Adding to this din was the rattle of 150 Canadian heavy machine guns, as they poured a barrage into the enemy's communication trenches.

With the wind and snow at their backs, men from the four Canadian divisions, fighting together for the first time, pulled themselves out of their assembly trenches and shell craters and began to pick their way across the shell-blasted no-man's-land and up the slopes of the ridge.

The 1st, 2nd, and 3rd Divisions were able to keep up to their barrage and gained their first objectives on schedule. The second line soon fell to the cheering Canadians, though resistance was beginning to stiffen. After a brief pause, the reserve troops came forward and passed through their victorious brothers as they were consolidating the newly won ground.

◄ *Looking over the crest of Vimy Ridge towards the Douai Plain.*

These fresh troops swept all before them, and by 3 p.m. the three divisions had taken all of their objectives.

For the hard-luck 4th Division on the left of the Canadian Corps the day had been going badly. Their main objective had been Hill 145 with its commanding view of the ridge and the Souchez Valley. Bristling with machine gun nests, it was proving to be an almost impossible position to take. Attack after attack went in, but only small portions fell to Canadian hands. Not until 10 April would this hornet's nest finally be cleared of the enemy.

With the capturing of Hill 145 on 10 April, the entire southern section of Vimy Ridge was placed in Canadian hands. There remained only The Pimple on the left to be taken. On the morning of 12 April, the 46th, 50th, and 44th battalions assaulted this heavily fortified knoll. Once again, the snow and wind were at the backs of the Canadians as they charged up the hill. However, the German's elite Prussian Guards were not caught napping. Coming out of their battered dugouts, they met the Canadians in no-man's-land and fierce hand-to-hand fighting took place in the driving snow. This time the men of the 4th Division would not be denied their victory, and soon the Prussian survivors were running down the far side of The Pimple. The Canadians calmly took aim and sniped many of the men before they could reach their shelters to the rear. By 8 a.m. The Pimple was captured and the entire Vimy Ridge belonged to these upstart colonials.

Unfortunately, the Vimy Ridge battle had only been allocated as a diversionary attack for the main Arras battle to the south. No plans had been made to follow up any victory which might occur on the ridge. So it was that the victorious Canadians could only sit in their positions and watch the routed enemy pull its guns and supplies out of harm's way and secure the new position to which it had retreated.

As it turned out, the main Battle of Arras achieved little or nothing. The French had suffered a humiliating defeat, and the British were able to make only small gains. The capture of Vimy Ridge had been the only real successful action in the overall battle. In supplying this victory, the Canadian Corps had suffered 10,602 battle casualties.

Chapter Seven

HILL 70 AND LENS

After the Canadian Corps' stunning victory at Vimy Ridge, they remained on the offensive with lightning trench raids and minor attacks. The Germans had withdrawn to the heavily fortified Hindenburg Line, and it was part of that trench system that the Canadians were hammering.

Meanwhile, to the north, Sir Douglas Haig was about to launch his long-cherished dream of smashing out of the Ypres Salient and clearing the enemy from the North Sea coast. To the south, the French Army, its morale broken from the strain of battle, mutinied and refused to take part in any new battles. This crisis within the French Army would continue until July 1918.

An important leadership change within the Canadian Corps took place on 9 June 1917 with the appointment of the Canadian-born Lieutenant General, Sir Arthur Currie as corps commander. After two and one half years of fighting in France and Flanders, the Canadian officers were finally receiving their just recognition.

Currie's first major operation as the new commander was planning for an attack on Hill 70 to the north of the city of Lens. If Hill 70 and its surrounding trench system could be taken, this would give the Canadians direct observation into the German-occupied city.

With the first streaks of dawn appearing on the 15 August and preceded by a barrage of high explosives and burning oil drums, men from the 1st and 2nd Divisions stormed into the

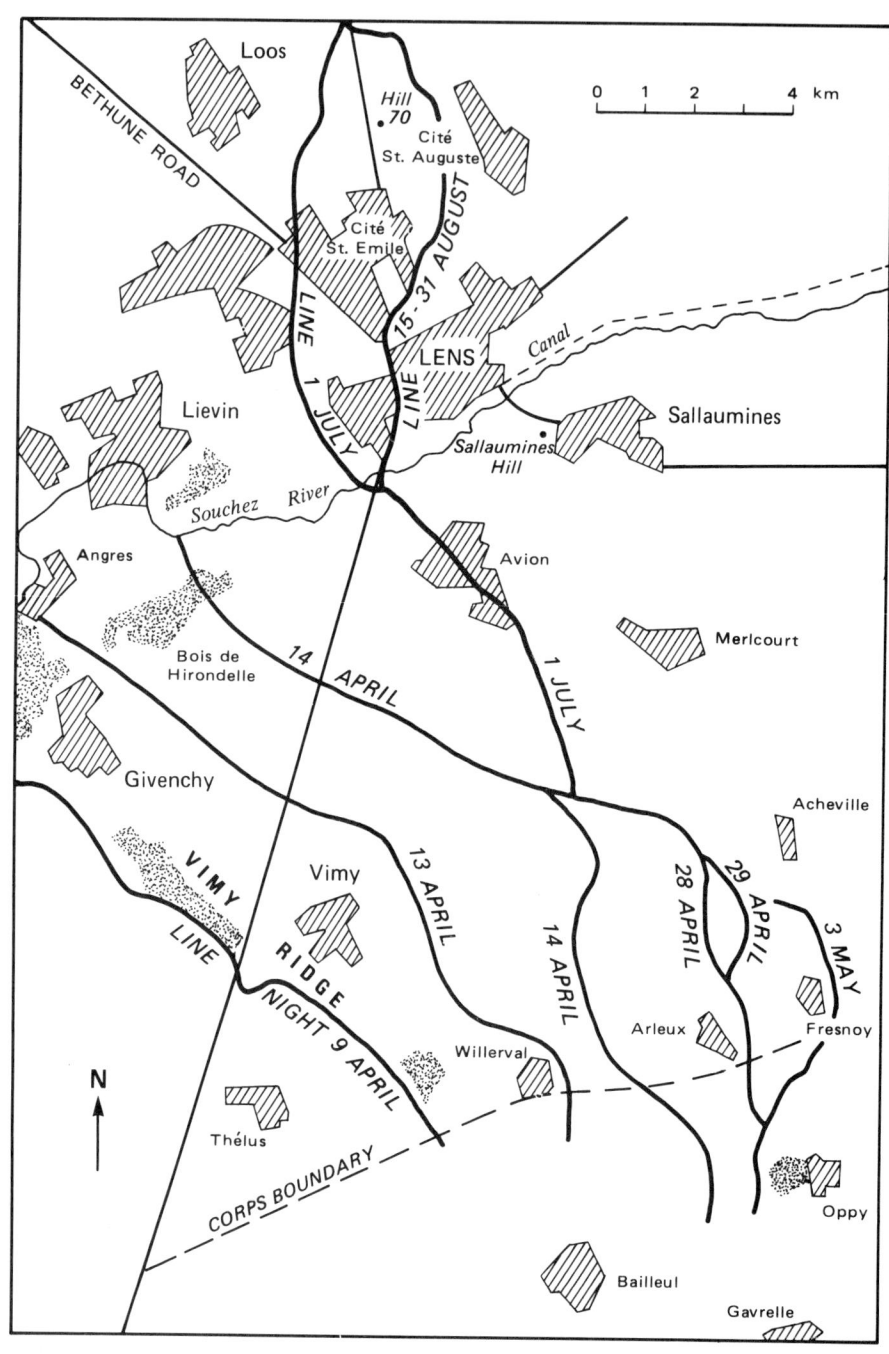

FROM VIMY TO HILL 70, APRIL - SEPTEMBER 1917
Canadian Corps' Advances

Field Marshall Sir Douglas Haig, Commander-in-Chief of the British Armies, inspects the 11th Canadian Infantry Brigade in February 1918. Haig is on the right.

ruins of the small coal mining villages in front of Hill 70. "The red light from the blazing oil, flashing and glittering on the long lines of bayonets was a sight to fire the imagination," quoted the 13th Battalion's historian.[1]

The fighting was fierce, as units from the two divisions fought their way through the maze of trenches, which cut their way through the rubble of the villages. A diversionary attack put on by the 12th Brigade of the 4th Division worked perfectly, since the enemy believed it to be the main attack towards Lens. This attack went off so well that the 4th Division received the brunt of the German artillery fire, thus enabling the 1st and 2nd Divisions to consolidate the positions they had captured. The German counterattacks on Hill 70 came almost immediately, but the Canadian gunners were more than ready and pounded

Lt. R.J. Steel in a support trench near Lens, May 1917. Note how puttees are wrapped.

the concentrations of Germans as they came over the top.

The remainder of the day was spent with small local attacks, as the Canadians straightened and fortified their newly captured positions. Though Hill 70 and most of the other objectives for

A German "pillbox" near the city of Lens, December 1917.

the day had been taken on schedule, the casualty lists showed that it had been a day of severe fighting. The Canadians had suffered 3,488 battle casualties.

The battle for Hill 70 and Lens soon became an artillery duel as well as an infantry battle. As the Canadians shelled the enemy, the Germans began retaliating with their newly introduced mustard gas shells. With hands and other exposed areas of their bodies blistered from this new gas, the gallant Canadian gunners fed their guns until they could no longer pick up a shell or pull the firing lanyard.

The infantrymen too were having their problems with this new gas, but they were to suffer yet even more as they began to encounter another German tool-of-war — the **flamethrower**. In the two days of fighting between 16 and 18 August, almost 1,400 Canadians became fire casualties.

Replacement gas mask for the hooded cloth mask. Photo taken in March 1917.

Between 21 and 25 August several attempts were made to take the city of Lens. At one point, Canadian patrols had actually entered the city, but these small parties were driven out by the enemy. On 25 August the battle for Hill 70 and Lens came to an end. Though the city had not been captured, the Canadians had furnished an important role by keeping several German divisions occupied in this area, while Sir Douglas Haig's armies in Belgium slugged their way towards the village of Passchendaele in the Ypres Salient.

The 10 days of continuous fighting had not been kind to the Canadian Corps. They suffered 9,198 casualties. Of these, 2,106 were caused by the enemy flamethrowers and 568 by mustard gas.

Chapter Eight

PASSCHENDAELE

"I got down on my knees in the mud and I prayed to God to bring me through. My whole life went before me and I couldn't see any future."[1] Private Pat Burns of the 46th Battalion had entered the wasteland of Passchendaele.

To the original 1st Division men, this area where they now found themselves in October 1917 was the same Gravenstafel Ridge area they had been driven from in April 1915. However, there the similarity ended, for now there was virtually nothing recognizable in this devastated landscape. Sir Douglas Haig's great plan of breaking out of the Ypres Salient had broken down into a yard-by-yard slugfest in the mire of the Stroombeek and Ravebeek valleys.

The conditions the Canadians had to fight in were almost indescribable. Artillery support was very poor, not because of bad gunnery, but because the guns were forever sinking up to their axles in the mud. After each shell was fired the gun had to be pried out of the muck and some semblance of sighting regained.

Before it even reached the guns, ammunition had to be transported by mules and then by hand for several kilometres along duck-board paths, which wound their way through the devastation and around shell holes. To make matters worse, the German gunners on the higher and somewhat drier ground had these pathways well sighted and continually blasted them with high explosives and shrapnel shells.

A man on a working party may have taken twelve hours

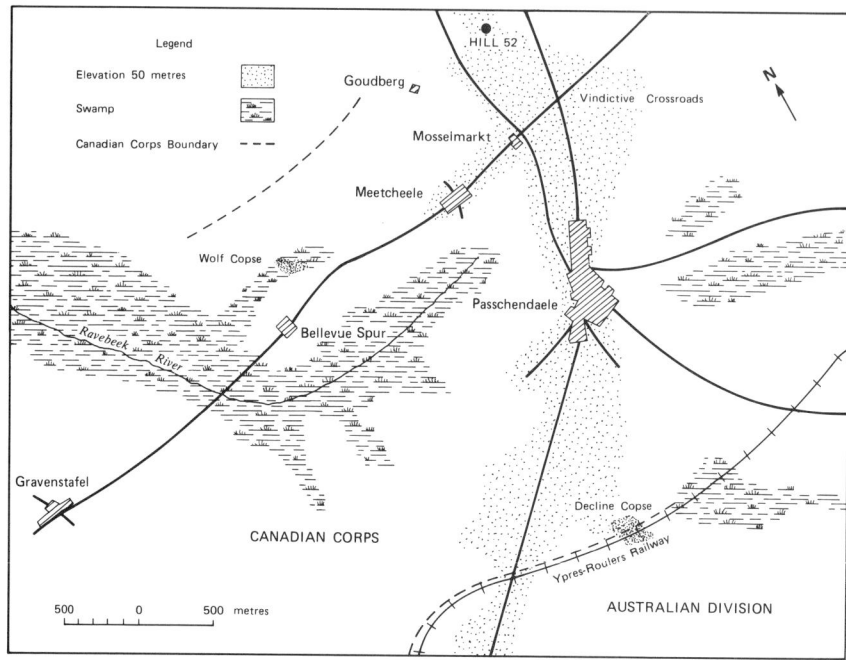

PASSCHENDAELE, OCTOBER - NOVEMBER 1917

to deliver his load of ammunition and return to the rear. If that man were wounded during his trek, he was more apt to drown in a shell hole or the mud, before he could be found and taken out to the rear.

In front of the Canadians the Germans held their positions, not in trench lines, but in well-sighted machine gun nests. Most of these posts were in the form of low, round concrete shelters, which reminded the men of the small circular tins in which medicinal pills were carried. Thus, to the British, the ANZACs*, and now the Canadians, these individual fortresses became known as pillboxes.

On 26 October the 3rd Division on the left of the Ravebeek and the 4th Division on the right went over the top at 5.40 a.m. The 46th Battalion on the extreme right, though suffering casualties from their own artillery barrage, waded through the

*NOTE: acronym for Australian New Zealand Army Corps.

Canadians carrying trench mats during the battle for Passchendaele. Note the wounded and prisoners in the background. November 1917.

bog and cleared Decline Copse, their final objective.

The 3rd Division initially did well and cleared several pillboxes on the Bellevue Spur. Unfortunately, the German artillery quickly found the range and literally began to blow the attackers back towards their jumping-off positions. Fortunately, one party from the 43rd Battalion held on to a pocket on the spur and the 9th Brigade were able to launch further attacks and stabilize their front.

On the right of the Ravebeek things began to go badly for the 4th Division. Strong enemy counterattacks slowly drove the exhausted remnants of the 46th Battalion out of Decline Copse and back to their original morning positions. It was not until the night of the 27/28 October that this area was secured by the 44th Battalion.

After a short breathing space, the Canadians were sent in

Enemy pillbox, Passchendaele 1917.

again, and at 5.40 a.m. on 30 October elements from the 3rd and 4th Divisions went to the attack. To the south of the Ravebeek the assault went well, even though the 85th Battalion lost nearly one half of its strength. The 72nd Battalion captured their objectives in front of the ruins of Passchendaeie and actually sent patrols into the village. However, they were soon pulled out.

To the left, or north of the Ravebeek, the 3rd Division plodded forward. The Princess Patricia's made quick gains, but were being cut to pieces by enemy machine gunfire. On their left the 49th, from Edmonton, was also under murderous fire, but was able to wade through the mud and keep abreast of the Patricia's. On the Division's far left the 5th Canadian Mounted Rifles, though at first bogged down in the swamp, soon made their way forward and had the enemy abandoning its kit while retreating. By late afternoon the Canadian attack had exhausted itself, and the survivors were ordered to dig in. To dig in meant to find a shell hole to crawl into and await further orders.

By 5 November the shattered 3rd and 4th Divisions had been relieved by their brothers from the 1st and 2nd Divisions. Like the men they had relieved, they too were aghast at the conditions of the battlefield which lay before them.

Perhaps fortunately, the infantrymen from the 1st and 2nd Divisions did not have much time to think about the horrible conditions they had entered into, for at 6 a.m. on 6 November they went over the top.

The 6th Brigade had taken over the right sector and their objective was the village of Passchendaele. On the left front the 1st Brigade was poised to capture the high ground near Mosselmarkt and Goudberg.

The attack went off like clockwork and, with the aid of an excellent artillery barrage, the men were able to capture most of the enemy's forward positions before its artillery could reply. The 28th Battalion, on the left of the 6th Brigade front, ran into withering machine gunfire and lost heavily, before clearing the enemy north of Passchendaele. Before 9 a.m. the elusive village was solidly in Canadian hands, as the 27th and 31st Battalions pushed through it and consolidated the area around the rubble of the town. The 26th Battalion from the 5th Brigade succeeded in securing the extreme right flank on time.

Meanwhile, on the 1st Brigade's front the attack, for the most part, went extremely well. It was only on the left flank that problems were encountered. Here, the 3rd Battalion was pinned down in a swamp in front of the German stronghold known as Vine Cottage. When at last the enemy's machine guns were silenced, the area was consolidated within two hours.

As in the Somme battles, so it was at Passchendaele — the Canadians would have to capture just one more section of high ground to finalize the autumn battles. This time, the area was the ridge north of Passchendaele which included Hill 52 and Vindictive Crossroads.

The 2nd Brigade using two battalions was to capture Hill 52 and the crossroads. The 4th Brigade attacking with its 20th Battalion would supply supporting cover on the right flank.

On 10 November in the pouring rain, the Canadians once

Bringing in the wounded, Passchendaele November 1917.

again went into action. Their first objectives were easily taken, and the 10th Battalion took over from the 7th and 8th Battalions of the 2nd Brigade and slowly pressed on. Unfortunately, the British unit on their left could not make any gains, and this left the 10th's left flank open to enemy fire. They were now a prime target, and the enemy blasted them all day. However, they grimly held on, and by evening their flank had been secured.

This final Canadian advance and the capture of the high ground north of Passchendaele brought the now named Third Battle of Ypres to an end. Sir Douglas Haig and his unimaginative staff had not been able to break out of the salient, although he had promised so many in the British government that he would. These battles of attrition, fought in such unheard of conditions, brought great suffering upon the men of the British and Dominion armies. For the Canadians, the two and one half

Destroyed allied tank in the wasteland of Passchendaele, November 1917. Note enemy shellburst to the left of the tank. ▶

16th Canadian Machine Gun Company holding a line of shell holes. Passchendaele, November 1917.

weeks spent in front of Passchendaele resulted in almost 16,000 casualties.

By the end of November 1917, the decimated Canadian Corps said good-bye to the Ypres Salient and returned to their familiar area in the Lens-Vimy front.

Nineteen seventeen was a year of splendid, though costly, victories for the Canadians. Vimy Ridge fell to them in April; Hill 70 in August; and they crowned the year with their capture of Passchendaele. These victories had not come easily, as their battle casualty list for these engagements grew to nearly 36,000. Their total casualties for all of 1917 totalled 75,000. And final victory seemed no closer.

Chapter Nine

THE BATTLE OF AMIENS

No major offensives took place during the winter of 1917/1918, but the men of the Canadian Corps did not find too many idle moments. Besides the inevitable trench raids and the constant patrolling, the infantrymen were employed in strengthening the Vimy sector defenses. All the signs pointed to a major German offensive in the spring of 1918, and the allies were sure that the enemy would attempt to retake the Vimy Ridge.

The storm burst on 21 March, but to the south of the Canadian Corps boundary. The 5th British Army was overwhelmed and routed out of the old Somme battle area and retreated towards the city of Amiens. Though making enormous gains, the Germans were unable to capture the city.

By 9 April the Germans had switched their assault to the Ypres sector and, within two weeks, had recaptured all of the ground that they had lost during the Battle of Passchendaele. Still, the Canadian infantry had not been attacked.

With their attacking troops exhausted in Flanders, the Germans turned to the south again and on 27 May launched their third and final assault. Though once again great breaches were made in the allied lines, the Germans could not keep up a concentrated attack. Within two weeks their offensive had ground to a halt, with no hope for a renewal.

In early August secret orders went out to move the Canadians south to Amiens, where they would spearhead the first major allied offensive of 1918. In order to deceive the enemy,

Working party bringing trench supplies and rations up to the front line. Note soldier with Lewis gun acting as anti-aircraft defence.

two Canadian battalions were sent north to the Ypres Salient, where they would let the Germans intercept their wireless communications. This was to lead the enemy into believing that the fresh Canadian units were mustering for an attack in that area. By now the Germans felt that wherever the Canadians were they could be sure of being attacked.

This ruse was partially successful, and by the night of 7 August the Germans were uncertain where the Canadian Corps was.

The Canadian infantry, along with their artillery and Cavalry Corps, were now ready for the attack on the morning of 8 August. Their position was about twelve kilometres east of Amiens, and they were to launch their attack on a five kilometre front (refer to map on page 16, letter **K**). On their left flank

Battle of Amiens. German prisoners carrying a wounded Canadian. Note tank advancing in the background. ▶

were the gallant Australians and on the Canadians' right were the French. The Canadian boundary on the right was the Amiens — Roye Road — and on the left the rail line, which ran east out of Villers-Bretonneux.

At 4:20 a.m. on 8 August more than 900 allied guns opened up a tremendous barrage and, preceded by over 100 tanks, the Canadians went into the attack — an attack which would prove to be their greatest victory of the war. With the **Horse Artillery** following in close support, the Canadian infantry poured through the enemy's defenses. Many Germans were captured before they could take up their positions and, in some cases, abandoned meals were found in captured dugouts.

Though pockets of resistance were encountered all across the Canadian front, these were soon overrun and captured. Entire German artillery batteries were captured, and specially trained Canadian gunners turned those guns on the fleeing enemy. The tanks, though rendering great assistance in some areas, for the most part found the going tough, and so it was the infantrymen who won the day.

The attack was going so well that long before noon the Canadian Cavalry was put into action. They enjoyed some successes, but the horsemen could find no way to defeat their old nemesis — barbed wire and machine guns.

By early afternoon the 4th Division, which had been held in reserve, joined in and the attack continued. The air was swarming with allied aircraft, as they spotted for the now mobile artillery and machine gunned the retreating enemy columns. After years of static warfare, it seemed that the entire front was now a great wave sweeping towards the enemy.

By early evening of the eighth the Canadians captured all of their objectives. In some places they advanced almost thirteen kilometres. General Erich von Ludendorff, the head of the German Army, would later write that "August 8th was the black day of the German Army in the history of this war."[1] The Canadians had captured over 160 artillery pieces, countless trench mortars and machine guns. They had also sent more than 5,000 captured Germans back to the prison cages.

On 8 August 1918 the Canadians incurred more than 3,800 casualties.

On the ninth the attack was resumed, but many delays and the lack of surprise made the advance somewhat shorter than the drive of the previous day. As the enemy's resistance began to grow stronger, the attack seemed to lose its momentum, and by the evening of the ninth the advance was halted, after an average gain of six kilometres.

The tenth and the eleventh saw the resumption of short hammer-like blows, as the Canadians found themselves in the old 1916 Somme battlefields. Old belts of rusted barbed wire and the crisscross maze of abandoned and overgrown trenches slowed and eventually stopped the advance.

By 20 August the Battle of Amiens came to a halt. The Canadians captured over 9,000 prisoners and 200 artillery pieces. Their casualties for the twelve days of fighting almost topped 12,000. General Currie, the Canadian Corps commander, called the Amiens battle, "This magificent victory." Magnificent as it was, the tenacious Germans had not had enough, and more victories would be needed before they would cry, "make it stop!"

Chapter Ten

PURSUIT TO CAMBRAI

With the Germans badly shaken after the Amiens battle, the allies could not afford to give them any rest. Rather than keep the pressure on in the old Somme defenses where the Germans were growing stronger, the allies planned their next major assault in the Arras sector to the north. The Canadians were again called on to spearhead this new attack.

The task laid out for the Canadians was to attack eastward from Arras astride the Arras-Cambrai Road (refer to map on page 16, letters **L** and **M**). Their main objective was to break through the Hindenburg and Drocourt-Quéant lines and push forward to the west bank of the Canal du Nord. These lines were two of the strongest enemy defensive positions on the western front, and unlike the Amiens battle there would be no chance for surprise during this nineteen kilometre advance.

On 26 August elements from the 2nd and 3rd Divisions swept out of their trenches at 3 a.m. Though the early hour of the attack surprised the enemy, the advantage did not last long, and soon the advancing Canadians were under heavy enemy artillery and machine gunfire. Casualties were steadily mounting, but the young Canadians fought their way forward and captured the strongly defended positions of Orange Hill, Chapel Hill, and Monchy-le-Preux.

For the next four days the Canadians were engaged in extremely heavy fighting, but continually moved towards their final objective. By the night of 30 August they had reached the outer defenses of the Drocourt-Quéant Line. If they could break

Canadians passing through a German barrage, September 1918.

through that line, they were sure that the Germans would pull back across the Canal du Nord.

Zero hour arrived on 2 September and, accompanied by a strong barrage, men from the 4th and 1st Divisions crept forward. "We were as close to the roaring barrage as we could possibly approach," wrote one Sergeant. "It was next to impossible to crawl through the wire, so we had to use paths which the enemy had left for his own convenience. A number of them [the enemy] tried to run back . . . . One of our machine gunners dropped with his gun and opened fire. They went down in a heap . . . .¹"

All along the front the Canadians punched through the belts of wire and engaged the desperate enemy. The machine gunners took a heavy toll, but eventually resistance collapsed and the objectives were met. The young men from Canada had swept through the Drocourt-Quéant Line and they cheered madly as they pursued the defeated enemy.

During the night the enemy withdrew to the opposite side of the Canal du Nord, and on 3 September the Canadian divisions advanced to the west bank of the canal.

The Canadian front would remain relatively quiet for the next three weeks, as plans were made for the assault across the dry canal. In the meantime, the British, French, and American armies were pounding the enemy all along the western front.

By 26 September the next phase of the Canadian pursuit was about to begin. They were to cross the dry section of the Canal du Nord, turn left and right, then sweep forward driving the enemy out of Bourlon Wood and the strongly fortified Marquion Line.

At 5.20 a.m. on the twenty-seventh the intricate barrage opened up, and assisted by a few tanks the Canadians charged across the canal. Immediately, they ran up against enemy machine gunners who were protected by massive belts of barbed wire. On many occasions that day the lumbering tanks proved their worth, as they crushed sections of wire and scattered the dug-in machine gunners. Though once again in retreat, the enemy was still able to inflict severe casualties on the attacking troops. As the men cleared the town of Bourlon and the Bourlon Wood, there arose a great cheer, for less than five kilometres away could be seen the enemy's major rail centre of Cambrai.

By 8 October the Canadians had pounded their way through the Marcoing Line and stood before Cambrai. On the ninth the attack went in.

Much to the surprise of these battle-weary men, they found the city nearly deserted, and a formal entry into Cambrai was made at 11 a.m. Two more short advances were made on the tenth and eleventh before the Canadians were relieved.

In the almost fifty days of continuous fighting, the Canadians had advanced for nearly thirty kilometres. Their own casualties since 22 August amounted to almost 31,000 all ranks. Again, it had been the enemy's gallant machine gunners who had caused most of the damage.

Chapter Eleven

CEASE-FIRE

On 17 October the Germans began their great retreat, which would not end until they had crossed the River Rhine into Germany. As for the Canadians, their role was to keep the enemy engaged under constant pressure.

As the Canadians pushed forward, they began to enter towns and villages which had been under German rule for over four years. Elated civilians met their liberators with kisses, cheers, and much wine. Young girls and old men were soon dancing in the streets, as the cheerful Canadians tried to keep some semblance of marching order.

The next major Canadian assault was the attack on the city of Valenciennes and its suburbs of Marly. This attack was to be carried out by battalions from the 10th and 12th Brigades, 4th Division.

At 5:15 a.m. on 1 November the rolling barrage began, and the troops followed closely behind it as it moved toward the city. On the left of the 10th Brigade all went well, but the right flank was under terrific machine gunfire. One Sergeant, who had earlier in the war been awarded the Distinguished Conduct Medal for bravery, wreaked havoc on the Germans that day.

Taking a Lewis gun [an automatic rifle] Sergeant Hugh Cairns quickly wiped out a nest of German machine gunners. Since his battalion was held up again, he opened fire and knocked over thirty of the enemy. This was not enough for the enraged Cairns who had become a one-man army.

Hugh Cairns, 46th Canadian Infantry Battalion. The last Canadian to be awarded the Victoria Cross in the First World War.

Firing from the hip, Cairns, now wounded, burst into the courtyard of a building from where enemy fire was coming. Almost immediately, sixty Germans threw up their hands to surrender. However, the German officer pulled out his pistol and

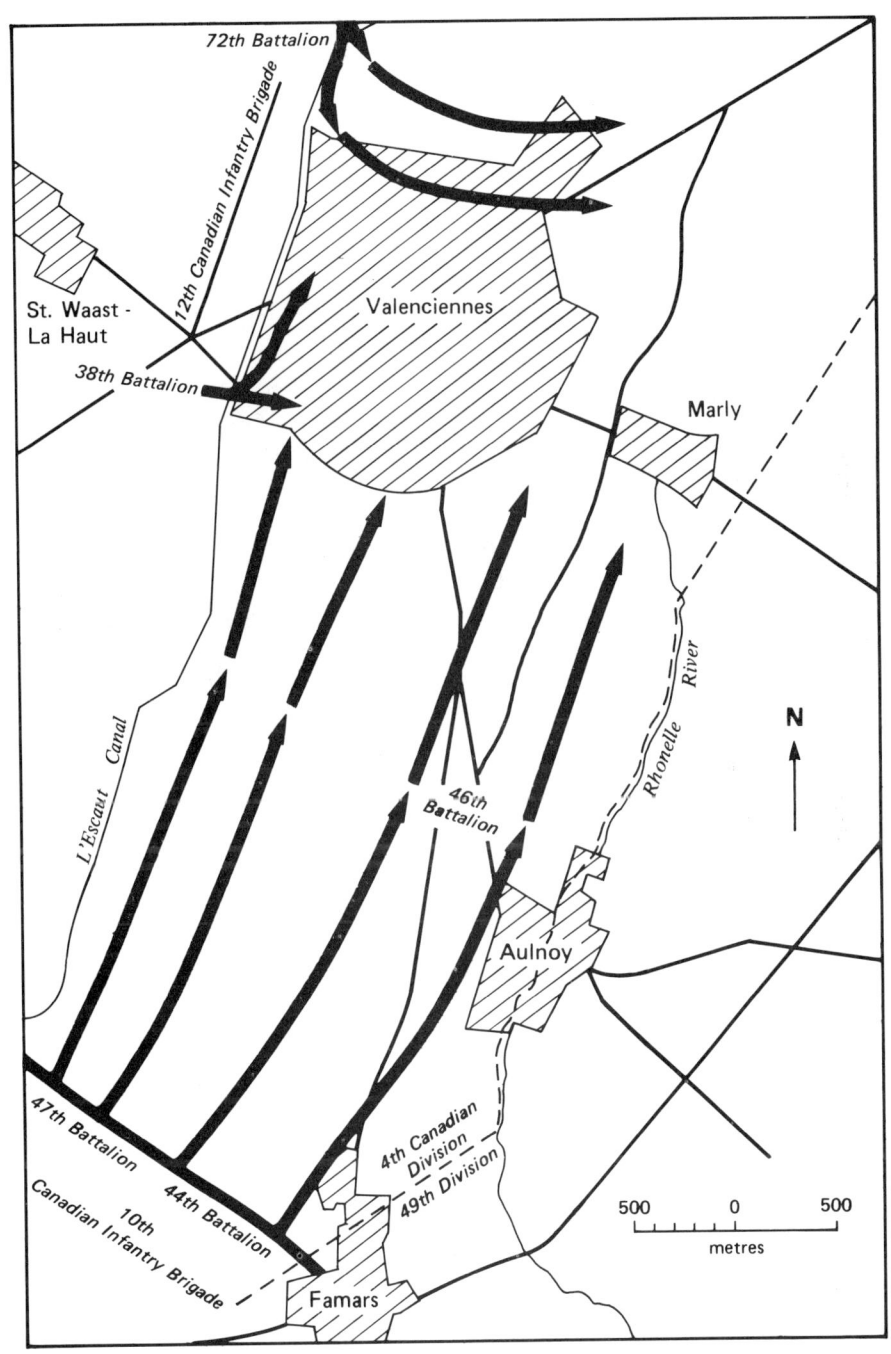

VALENCIENNES, 1 NOVEMBER 1918

A platoon from the 46th Battalion entering the western outskirts of Valenciennes on 1 November 1918. Picture was taken under fire.

shot Cairns. As the sergeant fell to his knees, he opened fire again, hitting the officer. In the turmoil, the Germans had rearmed themselves and returned the fire.

Cairns was hit twice again, but kept his Lewis gun firing until he collapsed. His section dragged him out of the chaos in the courtyard, but it was too late for Sergeant Hugh Cairns, for his wounds proved to be mortal, and he died the next day. For his great deeds of valour that day, Cairns was posthumously awarded Britain's highest award for valour — the Victoria Cross. This, in fact, was the last Victoria Cross to be awarded to a Canadian in the First World War.

In the meantime, the main attacks had been going successfully, and the 10th Brigade entered Valenciennes and captured sections of Marly. On 2 November the complete capture of Valenciennes and Marly was accomplished.

The enemy continued to retreat, with the Canadians in hot pursuit over the next week. Stubborn nests of resistance were quickly surrounded and captured, as the Canadian Corps maintained their relentless pressure.

Late in the evening of 10 November elements from the 42nd Battalion entered the town of Mons. By early morning the entire town had been cleared of the enemy, and by the 11 a.m. cease-fire the Canadians had advanced a few kilometres beyond Mons.

For the first time in over four years, there was not a sound of a gun to be heard along the entire western front. At 11 a.m. on the eleventh day of the eleventh month 1918 "The Great War" or "The War to End all Wars" ground to a halt.

During the war years, the Canadian infantry grew from a nucleus of 3,110 permanent soldiers to an army corps through which 619,636 men passed. Of those, 59,544 paid the supreme price and never returned to Canada's shores. The wounded infantrymen alone totalled over 125,000. The total fatal casualties suffered by Canadians in all branches of the armed forces numbered 60,661 — 9.28 percent of all those who had joined the colours.

In the four years spent in France and Belgium, the Canadians recaptured 130 cities, towns, and villages and reclaimed almost 1,000 square kilometres of allied territory. More than 45,000 Germans were captured by the Canadians, and to add to their booty they captured over 1,000 enemy artillery pieces.

For deeds of valour sixty-one Canadians were awarded the Victoria Cross — twenty-six posthumously. The Distinguished Service Order was awarded over 600 times; the Military Cross over 2,300 times. More than 1,400 people received the Distinguished Conduct Medal, while slightly over 7,700 Military Medals were presented. Almost 500 Meritous Service Medals went to Canadians and over 3,400 Mention in Despatches were recorded. Besides these British Empire awards, over 600 service people were decorated by foreign governments. Add to these the thousands of gallant deeds that went unrecorded, and it can be justifiably said that these young Canadians earned the respect of all those who encountered them.

Since the war, dedications of war memorials have taken place each year in almost every city, town, and village across Canada. At 11 a.m. on the eleventh day of the eleventh month, gatherings can still be found at these cenotaphs. It is now very rare to find any of these war veterans in attendance, as the intervening years have thinned their numbers and old age prohibits their participation in the march-pasts. However, the spirits of those men who marched away will forever be in the front ranks.

Epilogue

THE HOME FRONT

As a direct result of the war, the Canadian nation discarded most of its colonial status. Primarily an agricultural producing country prior to 1914, Canada expanded into a respected industrialized nation.

To meet the demands of the war effort, Canada's mining industry grew by leaps and bounds, as the need for new minerals to manufacture arms and ammunition grew. Old factories were converted to produce wartime products, while new technology was invented as the war's ravenous appetite for munitions, guns, and ships became insatiable.

Textile mills flourished in order to clothe the growing number of military personnel. Wheat, lumber, and meat producers enjoyed the benefits of the war market. Exports of flour and wheat doubled those of a decade before.

Women also enjoyed a new status on the home front, as they left their traditional jobs and replaced the men in the factories. It was a common sight to see women clothed in work coveralls clocking into munition factories and shipyards.

Perhaps the saddest issue of the war for Canada, besides the loss of so many young men, was the fracturing of the nation over the Military Service Act of 1917. The need for compulsory military service was deemed essential by the government in order that the depleted overseas battalions could be kept up to strength.

English-speaking Canadians and French-speaking Canadians held their own particular views on conscription and never, it seemed, could the two be reconciled. Years later the wound was still there, only to be opened wider when conscription was again at issue during the Second World War.

For the men returning home from the war in 1919, the changes must have been nearly overwhelming. The prewar backwater days were indeed a thing of the past. Canada had come of age.

CHAPTER QUESTIONS

Chapter 1

1. Was Canada involved in a foreign war prior to 1914? If so, when and where?
2. Canada is a member country in the North Atlantic Treaty Organiztion (NATO). What is the purpose of this organization and who are the other members?
3. Does Canada have any members of its armed forces stationed in a foreign country to meet its NATO commitments?
4. How does Canada's military commitment to NATO differ from its military commitment to the United Nations?
5. Name some of the countries where Canadian troops are, or have been, stationed as United Nations observers.

Chapter 2

1. The Ypres Salient was probably one of the most indefensible positions on the western front. The protection of the town of Ypres was more political than strategic. If you had been the commander of the allied forces would you have continued to hold the Salient at such great cost to human life or would you have withdrawn from the Salient and created a straight and more easily defended position to the west of the town of Ypres? Refer to map #2 for assistance.

Chapter 3

1. You are in a front-line trench in 1916 and have just completed your duties for the day. Compose a letter to someone at home describing your surroundings and a typical daily routine.

2. Why were trench raids and constant night patrolling in no-man's-land deemed so important by the Canadians?
3. Name two predominant innovations of World War I that were responsible for the creation of the static type of warfare.

Chapter 4

1. A lack of reliable and updated information coming from the battlefield was one of the biggest problems confronting the officers in charge of the battles. What methods of communications were used in the war and why were they so unreliable?
2. Because of government censorship, reports and casualty figures related in newspapers were somewhat less than factual. Why do you think the government censored reports coming out of the battle zones?

Chapter 5

1. The tank was probably one of the greatest surprise weapons of the war. Considering the battlefield conditions and the insufficient numbers of these machines, do you think it was wise to introduce this vehicle on the Somme in 1916? If you agree with its use, explain your reasons. If not, identify and explain your alternatives.
2. In the 1980s a war was fought in the mid-east between Iran and Iraq. Name the many similarities between that war and World War I.

Chapter 6

1. Explain why you believe Vimy Ridge was captured so quickly by the Canadians, whereas the French and the British had been unsuccessful in their attempts to drive the enemy off the ridge.
2. Of all the battles that the Canadian Corps participated in, Vimy Ridge seems to be the most revered of their many victories. Explain why you believe this to be so.

Chapter Questions 83

Chapter 7

1. When the Germans employed mustard gas and flamethrowers during the Hill 70 battle, the use of those weapons was decried as foul and inhumane. Do you believe that **rules** should be applied to war, or should the opposing countries be allowed to use any methods possible to gain victory?
2. Should the safety of the enemy civilians be taken into consideration when planning the strategy for war? Explain your answer.

Chapter 8

1. In November 1917 the British, supported by hundreds of tanks, attacked an area near the city of Cambrai. Their initial gains were great, but no reserve troops were made available to hold on to these gains. Within days, the Germans counterattacked and recaptured the entire area. Less than a month prior to this attack, the Canadian Corps was probably the allies' strongest unit on the western front. Imagine that you are the commander of the allied forces. Determine which tactics would be more useful. (1) A face-saving decision to use the Canadians in the horrid conditions of the Ypres Salient and hope that they can, at all cost, capture the high ground around the village of Passchendaele; (2) Keep the Canadians in reserve and use them in the upcoming battle near Cambrai; (3) None of the former: just strengthen all of their positions on the western front during the coming winter months. Justify your decisions.

Chapter 9

1. What important events took place in Russia in 1917 that led the allies to believe that the Germans would stage a massive attack on the western front in the spring of 1918?
2. Why was it so crucial for the Germans to gain a decisive victory and win the war in the spring of 1918?

3. What were the two main factors that gave the allies such a great victory at Amiens in August 1918?

Chapter 10

1. Explain the differences between the tactics used by the allies in the fall of 1918 and those used up to that time.

Chapter 11

1. From mid-October 1918 until the armistice on 11 November 1918, allied and German representatives were negotiating an end to the war. Clearly, Germany was near defeat. Do you believe that, with the imminent surrender by Germany the attacks launched by the allies were justified? If so, explain why you think it was so important to continue the attacks, knowing that many casualties would be incurred. If not, explain.
2. What was the name given to the peace treaty which ended the war and when was it officially signed?
3. Do you think that the conditions of surrender dictated in the peace treaty were directly responsible for the eventual rise of German nationalistic fervor and ultimately precipitated World War II? Explain.
4. Look into your family background to determine if you had relatives who participated in World War I. Write a brief story on their involvement in the war; i.e., when and where enlisted; what unit they enlisted with; battles fought in; wounds received; medals received.

GLOSSARY

BARRAGE – a curtain of artillery fire designed to destroy enemy trenches, machine gun posts, and barbed wire. A later innovation was called a "creeping" or "rolling" barrage. The attacking infantry would follow closely behind a moving barrage which slowly advanced toward and beyond the enemy's trenches.

BATTALION – an infantry unit consisting of approximately 1,000 men.

BATTALION BOMBERS – a specialist unit within the battalion trained in throwing hand grenades. These men were usually first to enter the enemy's trench during a raid and would clear dugouts and sections of the trench by lobbing these hand bombs down the dugouts or along the trench.

BILLETS – houses or camps where the troops stayed when out of the trenches

BREASTWORKS – usually a low wall of sandbags running along the forward edge of a trench. Also known as parapets. *(see illustration page 25)*

COMMUNICATION TRENCHES – trenches that ran forward from the reserve trench line through the support line and up into the front line. These were dug to enable movement between the three trench lines without exposing the men to enemy observation.

COMPANY – approximately 250 men, including cooks and signalers, made up a company. Four companies, lettered A, B, C, and D, made up a battalion. In 1914 a Canadian battalion consisted of eight companies of 125 men. This was changed by order on 16 January 1915.

DIVISION – Three infantry brigades comprised a division. Four infantry battalions comprised a brigade. Two Divisions comprised a Corps.

DUGOUTS – shelters originally dug into the side of a trench wall to provide shelter from rain or, to a lesser degree, enemy shellfire. As the war lengthened and the lines became more static, these dugouts were made much bigger and placed much deeper. The allied dugouts never became as elaborate as those built by the Germans. Enemy dugouts captured after 1916 were found to have electric lights, panelled walls, pictures, sofas; in one case, a piano had been placed in the officers' dugout.

FLAMETHROWER – a weapon strapped to the back of an infantryman that projected liquid fire from a canister.

GILL – a liquid measure equal to 1/4 pint (0.118 litre). This was usually issued to the men in the front line in the morning or just before going into an attack.

GUN CARRIAGE – A wheeled structure on which a cannon was mounted. Canada's main 'light' artillery was known as the "18-pounder" because the projectile fired from the gun weighed 18 pounds (8.17 kilograms).

HORSE ARTILLERY – a mobile artillery unit — usually "18 pounder" guns — pulled by teams of horses. These guns could be quickly pulled into action to assist the infantry. They could just as quickly be pulled out of action should the enemy get too close. Canada's horse artillery was known as the Royal Canadian Horse Artillery.

MOBILIZATION – Activating a nation's armed forces before proceeding to war.

MOPPING UP – capturing or silencing groups or individuals of the enemy who may have been bypassed during an allied advance.

N.C.O. – a non-commissioned officer i.e., Sergeant-Major, Sergeant, or Corporal. Though these men did not have a Kings Commission, their rank gave them authority over men of lower rank.

NO-MAN'S-LAND – a strip of land running between the allies' front trench and the German front trench. This area was generally patrolled at night by both parties, but was unowned and unoccupied by either.

PLATOON – companies were divided into four platoons of approximately fifty men per platoon. A battalion's platoons were numbered 1 through 16.

PUTTEE – a ten centimetre wide strip of cloth wound spirally about the leg from knee to ankle.

RESERVES – troops who were not on actual front-line duty. Usually the reserves were placed several kilometres behind the front lines and would be employed on working parties bringing supplies up to the front line at night. They could also be quickly called upon to give support to the front-line units, should the enemy launch an attack in their sector. While in reserves, the battalions were usually brought up to trench strength with the addition of replacement drafts and by men returning from leave or hospital.

STAR SHELL – a rocket-like flare fired from a hand-held gun and used at night to illuminate no-man's-land. Special coloured flares were used for signaling. Some flares would burst over no-man's-land and give just a brief illumination, while others were designed to release the flare on a small parachute, which would slowly drift down to earth giving a lengthier illumination period.

TRAVERSE – all trenches were dug in a zig-zag pattern. *(see illustration page 25)* This was done so to contain a shell burst to just a short section of trench. Also, if the enemy infantry were to get in the allied trench, they would not be able to shoot down an alley-like path.

When battalion bombers were raiding along a trench, they would throw a grenade into the next bay of the traverse, and then the infantrymen would run around the corner and mop up any survivors in the bay. This procedure would continue until the trench was cleared of the enemy.

APPENDIX "A"

Canadian battalions in the field listed under their respective divisions and brigades.

1st Canadian Division:
1st Brigade:
  1st Bn. (Western Ontario)
  2nd Bn. (Eastern Ontario)
  3rd Bn. (Toronto Regiment)
  4th Bn. (Central Ontario "Mad Fourth")

2nd Brigade:
  5th Bn. (Western Cavalry)
  7th Bn. (1st British Columbia Regiment)
  8th Bn. (Winnipeg "Little Black Devils")
  10th Bn. ("10th Canadians")

3rd Brigade:
  13th Bn. (Royal Highlanders of Canada)
  14th Bn. (Royal Montreal Regiment)
  15th Bn. (48th Highlanders of Canada)
  16th Bn. (Canadian Scottish)

2nd Canadian Division:
4th Brigade:
  18th Bn. (Western Ontario)
  19th Bn. (Central Ontario)
  20th Bn. (Central Ontario)
  21st Bn. (Eastern Ontario)

5th Brigade:
  22nd Bn. (French Canadian "Van Doos")
  24th Bn. (Victoria Rifles of Canada)
  25th Bn. (Nova Scotia Rifles)
  26th Bn. (New Brunswick "The Fighting 26th")

6th Brigade:
  27th Bn. (City of Winnipeg)
  28th Bn. (Northwest)
  29th Bn. (Vancouver "Tobin's Tigers")
  31st Bn. (Alberta)

Appendix "A"

3rd Canadian Division:
7th Brigade:
  Royal Canadian Regiment
  Princess Patricia's Canadian Light Infantry
  42nd Bn. (Royal Highlanders of Canada "The Black Watch")
  49th Bn. (Edmonton Regiment)

8th Brigade:
  1st Canadian Mounted Rifles
  2nd Canadian Mounted Rifles
  4th Canadian Mounted Rifles
  5th Canadian Mounted Rifles (These units had no horses in France & Belgium but fought as Infantry Units)

9th Brigade:
  43rd Bn. (Cameron Highlanders of Canada)
  52nd Bn. (New Ontario)
  58th Bn. (Central Ontario)
  60th/116th Bn. (60th replaced by 116th in April 1917)

4th Canadian Division:
10th Brigade:
  44th Bn. (Manitoba – redesignated New Brunswick in 1918)
  46th Bn. (South Saskatchewan)
  47th Bn. (British Columbia – redesignated Western Ontario in 1918)
  50th Bn. (Calgary)

11th Brigade:
  54th Bn. (Kootenay – redesignated Central Ontario 1917)
  75th Bn. (Mississauga)
  87th Bn. (Canadian Grenadier Guards)
  102nd Bn. (North British Columbians – redesignated Central Ontario in 1917)

12th Brigade:
  38th Bn. (Ottawa)
  72nd Bn. (Seaforth Highlanders of Canada)
  73rd/85th Bn. (73rd Royal Highlanders of Canada was disbanded in April 1917 and replaced by the 85th Nova Scotia Highlanders)
  78th Bn. (Winnipeg Grenadiers)

REFERENCE NOTES

Chapter One:
1. S.B. Fay, *The Origins of the World War* (New York, 1928), vol. ii, p.529.
2. Colonel G.W.L. Nicholson, *Canadian Expeditionary Force, 1914 - 1919* (Ottawa: Queen's Printer, 1962), p.5.
3. *Ibid,* p.12.
4. Ronald G. Haycock, *Sam Hughes* (Wilfrid Laurier University Press/National Museums of Canada, 1986), p.179.
5. Nicholson, *Canadian Expeditionary Force, 1914 - 1919,* p.30.

Chapter Two:
1. Colonel W.W. Murray, O.B.E., M.C., *The History of the 2nd Canadian Battalion* (Ottawa: The Historical Committee, 2nd Battalion, C.E.F., 1947), p.12.
2. R.C. Fetherstonhaugh, *The 13th Battalion Royal Highlanders of Canada 1914 - 1919,* 1925, p.45.
3. Nicholson, *Canadian Expeditionary Force 1914 - 1919,* p.90.

Chapter Three:
1. Murray, *The History of the 2nd Canadian Battalion,* p.68.
2. *Ibid,* p.70.
3. *Canada in the Great World War* (Toronto: United Publishers of Canada, 1919), vol. iii, p.229.
4. Canadian Corps Trench Orders, 21 October 1915.

Chapter Five:
1. *Letters From the Front* (Toronto: Canadian Bank of Commerce, 1920), vol. i, p.159.
2. James L. McWilliams, and R. James Steel, *The Suicide Battalion* (Edmonton: Hurtig Publishers, 1978), p.47.
3. *Ibid,* p.46.

Chapter Seven:
1. Fetherstonhaugh, *The 13th Battalion Royal Highlanders of Canada,* p.194.

Chapter Eight:
1. McWilliams and Steel, *The Suicide Battalion,* p.114.

Chapter Nine:
1. General Erich Ludendorff, *My War Memories* (London: Hutchinson, 1919), vol. ii, p.679.

Chapter Ten:
1. McWilliams and Steel, *The Suicide Battalion,* p.162.

SUGGESTED READING

Gas! The Battle for Ypres, 1915. J. McWilliams and J. Steel. Vanwell Publishing, St. Catharines, 1985.

Legacy of Valour. Daniel G. Dancocks. Hurtig Publishers, Edmonton, 1986.

My Grandfather's War. William D. Mathieson. MacMillan, Toronto, 1981.

No Man's Land. Victor W. Wheeler. Alberta Historical Resources Foundation, Calgary, 1980.

The Journal of Private Fraser. Reginald H. Roy, ed. Sono Nis Press, Victoria, 1985.

The Road Past Vimy. D.J. Goodspeed. MacMillan, Toronto, 1969.

The Somme. Lyn Macdonald. Michael Joseph, London, 1983.

The Suicide Battalion. J. McWilliams and J. Steel. Hurtig Publishers, Edmonton, 1978.

They Called It Passchendaele. Lyn Macdonald. Michael Joseph, London, 1978.

Vimy Ridge. Alexander McKee. Ryerson Press, Toronto, 1966.

ABOUT THE AUTHOR
R. JAMES STEEL

As a child, R. James (Jim) Steel loved listening to stories of his grandfather's adventures in the Boer War and World War I. A keen interest in military history borne out of this childhood experience has remained with him, through his service with the Royal Canadian Navy beginning when he was seventeen to today when this interest finds expression through writing. He is the co-author of *The Suicide Battalion* and *Gas! The Battle for Ypres, 1915.*

Married with two children and three grandchildren, R. James Steel currently resides in St. Catharines, Ontario, where he is employed with General Motors of Canada.

ABOUT THE PROJECT CONSULTANT
DON REVELL

Don Revell was born in Hamilton, Ontario and graduated from McMaster University in Honours Geography. He did post-graduate work in Environmental Studies at the University of Waterloo.

He is the author of several textbooks and is presently employed as a Consultant of Social Sciences and Outdoor Education for the Lincoln County Board of Education.

CREDITS

PHOTOGRAPHS

Author's p. 10, 54 National Archives of Canada (NAC) C 20240 p. 12 C 694 p. 13 PA 4460 p. 22 C 43985 p. 30 C 6984 p. 31 PA 262 p. 32 PA 86 p. 33 p. 36 C 43989 p. 39 PA 556 p. 42 PA 1446 p. 46 p. 48 PA 1128 p. 49 PA 2479 p. 53 PA 2329 p. 55 PA 928 p. 56 PA 2084 p. 59 PA 2210 p. 60 PA 2086 p. 62 PA 2195 p. 63 PA 2162 p. 64 PA 230 p. 66 PA 2951 p. 67 PA 3145 p. 71 PA 6735 p. 74 PA 3377 p. 75 PA 2367 p. 95

MAPS

Pg. 8 *Times History of War, Vol. I.* London: The Times, 1914, pg. 69

Pg. 16 Directorate of History. Ottawa: Department of National Defence.

Pg. 18 Directorate of History. Ottawa: Department of National Defence.

Pg. 27 Nicholson, Colonel G.W.L. *Canadian Expeditionary Forces 1914 - 1919.* Ottawa: Queen's Printer, 1962, pg. 123.

Pg. 34 Swettenham, John. *To Seize the Victory.* Toronto: Ryerson Press, 1965, pg. 111.

Pg. 38 *To Seize the Victory*, pg. 120.

Pg. 47 Author's.

Pg. 52 *To Seize the Victory*, pg. 179.

Pg. 58 Author's.

Pg. 75 Dancocks, Daniel G. *Spearhead to Victory.* Edmonton: Hurtig Publishers, 1987, pg. 189.

ILLUSTRATIONS

Pg. 19 Divisional Hierarchy, Author's

Pg. 23 Steel, R.E., Mining Operation

Pg. 25 Empey, Arthur Guy. "Front Line and Communication Trench" in *Over The Top*. N.Y.: G.P. Putnam and Sons, 1918, pg. 30.

Pg. 40 Empey, Arthur Guy. "Chemically Treated Gas Helmet" in *Over The Top*, pg. 190.

Pg. 41 Empey, Arthur Guy. "Overhead View of Typical Trench System" in *Over The Top*, pp. 94-95.

INDEX

Figures in bold refer to photographs, illustrations, and maps.

Albert-Bapaume Road 35
Amiens, Battle of 65,66,**67**,68,69,70; city of 65
Ancre Heights, Battle of the (phase three) 35,40
ANZACs 58
Arras, Battle of 50; sector 41,70
Arras-Cambrai Road 70
Atlantic Ocean 14
attrition 35,62
Aubers Ridge 21
Australia 34; Australians 68
Austria 9,11
Austro-Hungarian Empire **8**
Battalion, 1st 21,22,88; 2nd 15,21,23, 88; 3rd, Toronto Regiment, 23,61,88; 4th 35,88; 5th 26,27,37,88; 7th 26, 27,62,88; 8th 37,62,88; 10th 62,88; 13th, Royal Highlanders of Canada, 17,88; 16th Battalion, Canadian Scottish, 21,**22**,40,88; 20th 46,61,88; 21st 46,88; 22nd 37,88; 25th 37,88; 26th, New Brunswick, 37,61,88; 27th 30,37,61,88; 28th 30,61,88; 29th 30, 88; 31st 30,61,88; 42nd, Royal Highlanders of Canada, 9,37,77,89; 43rd 59,89; 44th 43,50,59,89; 46th 10,43, 50,57,58,59,**74,76**,89; 49th 60,89; 50th 44,50,89; 72nd 60,89; 85th 60,89
Belgium 11,15,56,77
Bellevue Spur 59
Borden, Sir Robert (Prime Minister) 12,**13**
Bosnia 9
Bourlon, town of 72; Wood 72
Brielen 17
Brigade 1st 61,88; 2nd 21,40,61,62,88; 3rd 21,35,40,88; 4th 61,88; 5th 37, 61,88; 6th 61,88; 7th 31,37,89; 8th 31,37,89, 9th 59,89; 10th 43,46,73, 76,89; 11th 43,53,89; 12th 43,53, 73,89
British Army 9,14,62
Burns, Private Pat 57
Cairns, Sergeant Hugh 73,**74**,76
Cambrai 70,72
Canadian Corps **27**,28,29,44,50,51, **52**,56,64,65,66,69,77

Canadian Mounted Rifles, 1st 33,46; 4th 37; 5th 33,60;
Canal du Nord 70,71,72
Cavalry Corps 66,68
Chapel Hill 70
Courcelette 35,36,37,39,40
Currie, Lieutenant General Sir Arthur 51,69
Decline Copse 59
Divisions, 1st 13,15,17,19,20,21,22,29, 31,34,35,49,51,53,57,61,71,88; 2nd 24,29,30,**31**,35,36,37,49,51, 53,61,70,88; 3rd 13,29,31,33,35,36,49,58,59,60, 61,70,89; 4th 34,35,41,43,44,46,50,53,58,59, 60,61,68,71,73,89;
Douai Plain 45,**48**,49
Douve River 26
Drocourt-Quéant Line 70,71
Duck's Bill 23
duckboards 57
Ellis, Private Victor **10**
England 11
Ferdinand, Archduke Franz **8**
Festubert 21
Flanders 51,65
Flers-Courcelette (phase one) 35,39
France 11,14,15,34,51,77
French Territorial Division 17
Frezenberg Ridge **19**
gas, chlorine attacks 17,19; helmet **40**; mask **56**; mustard 55,56
Gaspé 14
German Army 15,68
Germany 9,10,11,12
Givenchy 21
Goudberg 61
Gravenstafel Ridge 57
Haig, Sir Douglas 51,**53**,56,57,62
Hill 52 61; *Hill 60,61,62* 31; *Hill 70* 51,**52**,53,54,55,56,64; *Hill 145* 50
Hindenburg Line 51,70
Hughes, Sir Sam (Minister of Militia) **12**
Italy 11
Lee-Enfield rifle 18,20,21
Lens 51,53,**54**,**55**,56

Lens-Vimy Front 64
Lewis Gun 66,73,76
Ludendorff, General Erich von 68
Machine Gun Company, 16th
 Canadian **64**
Maple Copse 33
Marcoing Line 72
Marly 73,76
Marquion Line 72
Messines 26
Military Service Act 1917 79
Monchy-le-Preux 70
Mons 9,77
Mosselmarkt 61
Mount Sorrel 31,**34**
Mouquet Farm 35,37
Neuve Chapelle **15**
Neuville St. Vaast 45
New Zealand 34
Non-Permanent Active Militia 12
North Sea 51
Notre Dame de Lorette Spur 45
Orange Hill 70
Ovillers 37
Passchendaele 35,56,57,**58,59,60**,61,
 62,63,64,65
Permanent Force (Permanent Active
 Militia) 11
La Petite Douve Farm 26
Pillbox **55**,58,59,**60**
Pimple, The 45,50
Ploegstraat 24,
Plymouth 14
Pozières 35,37,43
Princess Patricia's Canadian Light
 Infantry (the Pats) 13,19,20,26,33,
 37,60,89
Prussian Guards 50
Quebec 13
Ravebeek Valley 57,58,59,60
Rhine River 73
Ross rifles 13,18,21,**32**
Royal Canadian Regiment 9,89

Roye Road 68
Russia 10,11
Salisbury Plain 14
Sanctuary Wood 31
Sarajevo **8**,9
Serbia 9
Somme, 36,**39**,41,43,44,61,65,69,70;
 Battles of 34,35,**38**
Souchez, River 45;
 Valley 50
South Africa 34
Southampton 14
St. Eloi, craters **30,31**; town of 29
St. Lawrence River 14
Steel, Lieutenant R.J. **54**
Stroombeek Valley 57
sugar refinery **36**
Thiepval Ridge (phase two) 35,39,40
trench raids 26,27
trench mats **59**
Trench, system **41,42**; Candy **36**;
 Desire 43; Fabeck Graben 37,39;
 Hessian 39,40; Kenora 39;
 Regina 39,40,41,43,44;
 Sugar 36;
Triple Entente 11
Triple Alliance 11
Valcartier 13
Valenciennes 73,**75,76**
Victoria Cross 74,76,77
Villers-Bretonneux 68
Vimy Ridge 21,45,**46,47,48,49**,50,51,
 52,64,65
Vindictive Crossroads 61
Vine Cottage 61
Westminster, Statute of 11
western front **16**,24,28,70,72,77
Ypres, 31,33,65; Battles of,
 Second 19,20; Third 62; city of
 17,19; Salient 17,**18**,29,31,**33**,35,
 43,51,56,57,62,64,66
1st Divisional Headquarters 17
5th British Army 65